FINALLY FREED & JOY-FILLED

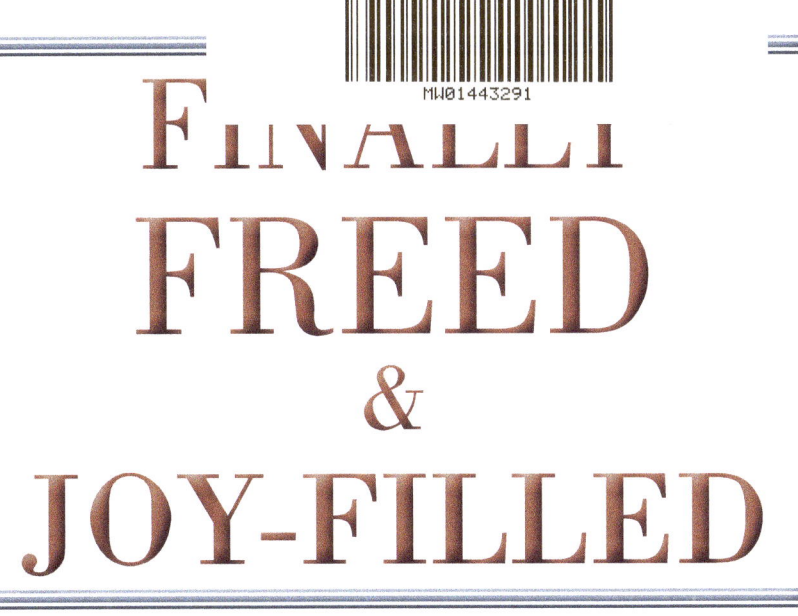

The Seven Foundational Footers You Need to Generate Emotional Wealth

Regrets, fear, and anxiety suck! Living a joy-filled life should never be optional for anyone. Dare 2B More…Joy-Filled!

LAURA WILLIAMS

ISBN 978-1-63903-901-2 (paperback)
ISBN 978-1-63903-903-6 (hardcover)
ISBN 978-1-63903-902-9 (digital)

Copyright © 2019 by Laura Williams

All rights reserved. No part of this publication may be reproduced, distributed, or transmitted in any form or by any means, including photocopying, recording, or other electronic or mechanical methods without the prior written permission of the publisher. For permission requests, solicit the publisher via the address below.

Christian Faith Publishing, Inc.
832 Park Avenue
Meadville, PA 16335
www.christianfaithpublishing.com

"InJOYou" and "DARE 2B MORE…" are registered trademarks of InJOYou, LLC

Printed in the United States of America

Contents

Introduction 5
Prelude 9
    DARE 2B MORE… 9
The Backstory 17
    My Journey 17
    You Are Never Ready 24
    Free Falling 28
Chapter 1 35
    Unfulfilled to Joy-Filled 35
    A Love Letter to You 35
    The Happiness Drug! 42
Chapter 2 49
    DARE 2B MORE…Living 49
Chapter 3 57
    InJOYou, Inc. 57
    The "Business" of Your Life 57
    Reactive vs. Responsive 60
    The Business Viewpoint 62
Chapter 4 69
    Leadership 69
    God is My CEO 72
Chapter 5 81
    Ecosystem 81
    The Ecosystem of InJOYou, Inc. 84
Chapter 6 91
    The Seven Foundational Footers 91
    The Rearview 94

Chapter 7	99
Footer 1—Faith	99
Chapter 8	111
Footer 2—Forgiveness	111
The Earth Quaked	112
What Forgiveness Is	124
What Forgiveness is *Not*	129
Chapter 9	135
Footer 3—Accountablility	135
Chapter 10	147
Footer 4—Dream	147
Dream Big! Dream Bold!	152
Chapter 11	157
Footer 5—Intentional Choice	157
Chapter 12	169
Footer 6—Acceptance	169
Chapter 13	177
Footer 7—Mentors	177
Chapter 14	185
Summary—ROI	185

Introduction

This book is dedicated to the overcomer in you!

"How" is a word that can both cripple and empower. How can I want something I have never once dared to dream? How can I dream of becoming a person I have never met? How do I build a life of joy when all I have ever known is one of pain and regret? How can I build a joy-filled life when I have no frame of reference? How can I change my reality when I made every mistake that created it? These questions haunted me most of my life. I knew I wanted something different—something better—but I did not know how to obtain it.

I felt like everywhere I looked was void of the people, places, and things that could teach and guide me to build a life of more joy than regret. I had more excuses than the ocean has water for why a joy-filled life was not in the cards for a girl like me. Believing in the lies that I was not enough, could not be enough, and would never be enough was holding my joy hostage. It wasn't my circumstances, toxic upbringing, abusive marriage, or lack of pedigree that had held my joy hostage for over forty years. However, these were the excuses I claimed to remain in neutral. No, it was not any of those things; it was my own self-sabotaging and self-limiting beliefs that led to one poor choice after another. I did not know it, but I had permitted myself to live as if I were merely an employee in building the business of my life—one with no voice and no other choice.

How I wish someone would have told me that God created us to be the chief-operating officer in the business of our lives. Or that our purpose was to intentionally build our lives to manufacture and distribute a product of joy for God, others, and ourselves. Had I known from childhood that how we live each day decides the legacy we leave—had I understood the gravity of that reality—I would not have squandered the precious minutes of my life, building a legacy of more regrets than joy. Had I known that there is a monumental difference between joy and happiness, I would not have wasted time chasing something as fleeting and elusive as happiness.

I needed a new perspective before I could free myself from the chains of victimhood. A series of events, including a near-death illness, difficult divorce, kids leaving for college, and my mother's sudden passing, provided that new perspective. I had to own that the only thing holding my joy hostage, crippling my relationships, and limiting my dreams were my values, beliefs, and choices. I was accountable for my reality.

My regrets and pains, disappointments, and failures were like unopened gifts. I just didn't know it! My past failures, regrets, hurts, and disappointments equipped me with a set of priceless tools which unlocked every chain binding my gifts, strengths, and talents, and ultimately, set my joy free!

I wrote this book because living a joy-filled life should never be optional! No one should wait forty-six years like I did to realize their best life. Far too many of us settle for a lukewarm, passionless life of being uncomfortably comfortable. Why do we settle for less than is possible? Why do we resign to meeting each new day with dread instead of enthusiasm and gratitude? Why do we settle for woulda, shoulda, and coulda when we have the power of choice to define and build the legacy, we most want? For most of us, the answer is we do not know how to answer the question "how?" It is often easier to believe the web of lies created by others, us, and our circumstances than it is to imagine something better. This tangled web of lies restricts your self-esteem, confidence, and beliefs that you are not just capable but deserving of a life that overflows with an abundance of joy. You are meant and deserve to know joy—to live boldly, act boldly, and be finally freed and joy-filled.

Does that sound impossible? Does that seem like a lofty fairytale—something reserved for others but not you? There was a time when I thought so too, but no longer! There are three things you need to change your trajectory from unfulfilled to joy-filled—faith, desire, and a blueprint! I cannot give you desire nor faith, but what I can give you is a blueprint!

Across the pages that follow, my goal is to equip you with the tools that I acquired over forty years of getting it wrong before I finally got it right. These tools, when applied, will empower you to be non-negotiably you! God created you to know joy—to dream, build, live, and leave a legacy of joy for God, others, and yourself! You are enough; you have always been more than enough! I hope that I can disrupt your trajectory from living a life that is unfulfilled to joy-filled. If I can, then every pain and regret, once mine, was worth it! It is time for you to stop living like an employee in the creation of your story. Take your rightful place as the COO in the business of your life, that of InJOYou, Inc., and get busy building it to manufacture and distribute a product of joy! In the pages that follow, I will share with you how to clear the ground, poor the seven foundational footers of a joy-filled life, and start building the business of your life—InJOYou, Inc. to maximize joy and minimize regrets. The reality is that I can equip you with the tools, but if you are not willing to grind it out and do the work, the tools will hold no value for you. However, if you choose to use these tools every day, I can promise you that your life will exponentially change for the good.

Let the question "How?" empower you to be finally freed and joy-filled!

Shop our online gift store @ www.Injoyou.com for motivational products like journals, tumblers, t-shirts, hoodies, shoes, and more. These products are designed to encourage and support you as you DARE 2B MORE... JOY-FILLED!

Prelude

DARE 2B MORE…

Dare 2b more…is a challenge to you and for you. It is not easy. As an empowerment coach, clients often tell me, "I keep trying, but it is just so hard" or "I try, but I keep getting knocked down." My gut reaction to this mindset is always the same:

First, the problem is your belief system; you have bought into the lie that things are supposed to be easy. No one ever promised your life would be easy! The second problem is you are trying rather than doing. Trying does not move you forward! Taking action does! The third possibility is you have deemed yourself a "victim." Victim mentalities are perpetuated by excuses but can be overcome through accepting personal accountability. If things are always hard (in the light of a truth that your efforts continually fail to move you forward), I will bet money you are getting a payoff for staying the course! If you were not, then your efforts would yield more favorable results.

A victim mentality allows you to blame others for your circumstances—to absolve you of any accountability, responsibility, or motivation for changing your beliefs, habits, or circumstances.

A dare 2b more…life means making choices so intentional your dreams have no other choice than to come to fruition. But more importantly, it means building and living your life on purpose with purpose—to dream, design, build, live, and leave a legacy of joy.

I have had the amazing good fortune to travel to a great many places. Along the way, I have met people from all walks of life, each with incredible, inspiring, and unique stories. Throughout my countless adventures, I have met endless streams of people in taxis, airports, restaurants, and hotels who have changed me in some small way. This is ironic, given I do not easily meet people in my own backyard. Many have remained in my circle of friendship long after we parted. Most of these happenstance friendships developed while I was flying.

I have always had an affection for airplanes and flying. In my youth, I searched the skies, hoping to see a passing aircraft. I imagined myself on board, traveling to wondrous places, meeting all kinds of interesting people, and witnessing the sheer beauty of God's creation. Mostly though, I imagined all the heartaches I could escape if only I could fly away. Still today, when I hear the increasing roar of a nearing plane, I look up, search, and wonder much the same. Sometimes, when my spirit feels overwhelmed, I find myself sitting under a nearby flight path, watching the planes come and go, still with curiosity and wonderment about the stories belonging to those onboard.

As you can probably surmise, one of my more favorite places is the airport. Yup! It is true! I genuinely love every part of the airport experience, even the tedious wait at baggage claim. In all truthfulness, that might be one of my more favorite parts of air travel. Crazy, I know! However, it is in baggage claim where the real stories play out.

I have observed the long-awaited soldier finally returning home, the moms and dads hugging their child just returning from college, the young adult embarking on his first adventure, the couple reuniting, the newlyweds living out their first day of married life, the grieving family members finally connecting to those they love, or the consultant signing or losing his first deal; emotions are genuine. These emotions are raw and rarely held back. I love watching the human condition from the baggage claim because no one is looking around to see who is watching or judging them. People allow themselves a moment of emotional freedom.

Back to why I revere the airport experience; it is because of the stories contained within the corridors, each of immanent significance! Every traveler knows exactly where they are going and why. They made a plan, booked a ticket, and showed up, ready to go. Even the rare person who randomly wanders into the airport without a plan still must choose a destination, book a ticket, and get on the plane. If they don't choose a destination, grounded in the airport is where they will remain. They have no other choice than to make a choice, stay on the ground, or choose a destination and go! Seems obvious, right! The point is that because the traveler's *why* is so clear, they don't struggle to complete their mission; they are intentional, decisive, and focused on bringing their goals to fruition.

The second reason I love air travel unfolds during the actual flight. People are willing to open up and have real conversations. I have a theory about why, although I have never really tested it. Perhaps knowing they likely won't see this other person again holds the space to speak freely and confidently. Maybe they desire connectivity, attention, or companionship. Whatever the cause, sitting three inches from your travel companion certainly creates plenty of opportunities to chat for a spell!

When you think about it, the cabin of an airplane truly is a brilliant platform for communicating. In general, people are more or less forced to adhere to that age-old advice, "If you can't say something nice, then don't say anything at all." Most are not willing to forfeit what they want most—to disembark and go about their business, to engage in verbal warfare with a complete stranger. I guess the notion of disembarking in handcuffs is generally reason enough for passengers to quickly deescalate any potential tensions. Putting aside the obvious, what I have found to be true is that when I've allowed myself to be open to engaging with my fellow travelers, I walked away different from when I first sat beside them. You simply never know if the person who plops down beside you does so because Jesus orchestrated a divine appointment for one or both of you.

Have you read the book *The 5 People You Meet in Heaven*? If you have not, you should! My variation of that book would be titled *The 5 People You Meet on Airplanes*. Chance encounters with complete strangers has significantly impacted my worldview on a variety of topics!

Take for example, Dorothea from Barbados! A simple acknowledgment of her warm "hello" led to a three-and-a-half-hour conversation—one that would later prove instrumental in my writing this very book.

She was a legendary, world-renowned shell artist married to a famous quartet singer. She was kind, humble, and enthusiastic about her life. Her joyful nature alone was more than enough to inspire me.

My daughter, who normally is only captivated by her cell phone, and I listened intently as Dorothea told us stories of her grand adventures. Hers was a fairy-tale-like life that made me hunger for a different life—a better life. Of the things she shared with us that day, there was one sentence that inspired real change in me.

At the time of our conversation, I was in the midst of an interview project. I was on a quest to validate my theory that at our core, most people really do share the same basic hopes, dreams, fears, and regrets. *What is the greatest regret of your life?* was one of the ten questions I asked of my interviewees.

Dorothea's answer was like seeing a mountain, covered by fresh fallen snow—Brilliant! "I don't give consideration to regrets. I have *no* regrets beyond just this one… As my husband laid dying in my arms, he uttered his last words, but my mind failed to record them. I can't recall the last words spoken to me by the love of my life, just before Jesus called him home. That would be my only regret in my eighty-six years."

This amazing woman sitting next to me lived eighty-six years so intentionally she genuinely felt no regrets. Over the next few minutes my mind replayed her words "no regrets" over and over again. Two more questions came to the forefront of my thoughts. I wanted to know *how* she had lived her eighty-six years so intentionally that regrets never had a home in her soul. I also wanted to know how, moving forward, I could live my life so that regrets no longer had a home in mine. So…I asked her, "How is it that you have had no regrets across your eighty-six years?"

Dorothea replied, "I had wonderful parents who taught me to love and trust the Lord. I have always lived as I chose. I selected and married the right man. I have always sought what was possible, and I never failed to be in gratitude, regardless of plenty or want!"

I thought, *Well, folks, there you have it!* I felt as if she had given me a magic scroll containing the secret of life. It read like this:

> *Intentionally declare this life is yours for living, not surviving.*
> *Live each day as you choose but always with*
> *gratitude for all that you've already received.*
> *Finally, choose your values and your company very wisely;*
> *For they will become the memories that tell the tale of your journey.*

Another such person who changed my perspective was Leroy, a ninety-four-year-old man ironically also from Barbados, but now a long-time resident of Baltimore, Maryland.

My boyfriend and I were waiting in the security line at BWI airport when we first discovered Leroy. He was alone in the airport and struggling to carry a very heavy, tattered, and torn duffel bag. I graciously volunteered my boyfriend to carry it for him. As it turned out, we were all going to the same gate. He was also traveling to Barbados, so I decided we would adopt him for the trip.

I planned to deliver him safely to his loved ones on the other side! During the hours we spent together, Leroy shared stories of his life. He had a life of plenty as a Barbadian. However, the past twenty-five years in Baltimore had not been as easy for him.

He came to Baltimore with his wife and seven children, four of which were not of his blood, although he proudly claimed them as his own. In Baltimore, Leroy was victimized again and again. He experienced racism, crimes of hate, violence, robbery, and more. He was a mechanic who had proudly and patiently worked his way from employee to owner. He spoke humbly of the life he and his lovely wife (may God rest her soul) built together.

Leroy shared an unlimited account for the reasons he ought to be, filled with anger, bitterness, and resentments. Lord knows, anger welled-up inside of me just hearing his stories. Yet, despite being horrifically victimized by numerous people, I noted that his demeanor remained kind, joyful, grateful, and loving. His eyes reflected his genuine nature. He had every reason to be angry, but there was not a trace of it in him. This stranger was teaching me things I did not realize I still needed to learn about gratitude, love, humanity, drive, and staying power. Perhaps, I was open to hearing all he did not say rather than just being entertained by what he did. Leroy was teaching me the value of having a forgiving heart in a broken world.

I asked him about his recipe for remaining humble and kind when his community had shown him little kindness or compassion. In his soft-spoken way, he stared into my eyes and said, "I count my God-gifted blessings each, and every day. I never stop working hard to provide the 'provision of care' I want for my family!" I had never heard anyone frame the words care and provision together the way he just had. His mission was to work hard so that he could provide *care* for others! Leroy gave me a second secret scroll. This one read:

In all situations, give thanks for the gifts that
God himself, has bestowed upon you.
Use those gifts intentionally to work and earn the provision of
CARE you most desire to bestow upon all whom you love.

The next time you fly, do not be so anxious to tune out your travel companions! *Tune in!* Otherwise, you may be cheating yourself and others of receiving or giving a life-changing gift you weren't expecting!

I hope you will take from this book a new perspective about who you are, your worth, and your superpower to realize the joyous life God always intended for you to experience. Living a joy-filled life should never be an option. My greatest desire is that by equipping you with my tools, the tumultuous journey that was mine will not be yours.

You have God-given talents and strengths you are meant to tap into, develop, and share. Every day, God grants you another breath is another opportunity to dare 2b more…, more than you were the day before! Regardless of where you currently are in your life, if you feel a sense of restlessness that cannot be tamed or you just feel "stuck," then I invite you to keep reading. My hope is to unveil all the beautiful possibilities for you to build a joyous life. If you are willing to adjust your perspective from that of an employee to that of a business executive, and to have a little faith, and a whole lot of accountability, then you can build a life that is sustained by joy just like I have. My desire is to equip you with the tools to change your trajectory from unfulfilled to joy-filled.

Are you ready to DARE 2B MORE…JOY-FILLED?

THE BACKSTORY

MY JOURNEY

Do you greet each day with a spirit of joy, excited by the dawning of the new day? Have you ever asked yourself, "Is this as good as it gets?" Have you ever looked around the landscape of your life and thought, "How did I get here? What is my purpose? What am I doing?" Have you ever felt as if you were a visitor in your own story—as if you were just *stuck*? You are not alone!

If you are anything like I was, joyful is not how you greet each new day. Most days, I woke reminded of the obstacles, challenging people, and drama-consumed situations waiting just beyond my bedroom door—each poised to steal my joy. Lying there on my comfy bed, I would wonder what my nemesis would be today. Truth be told, I got out of bed everyday exhausted, wanting only to go back to sleep.

This was not exactly a stellar outlook for a person whose only desire was joy and peace. I wanted to feel the warm sun on my face, to take in the beauty and harmony of nature and, mostly, to help those I love to discover their most joyous life. I know that sounds a bit lofty and poetic, but it really was all I wanted. Fine…in the interest of no BS, I also wanted a little extra money in the bank to fund my poetic and lofty ideologies! Unfortunately, my reality stole more joy than it produced. My heart held a picture of what I wanted my life to look like.

Unfortunately, my reality was a constant reminder that the picture in my imagination was little more than a Hallmark movie script. My relationships were challenging at best. My career was up and down and sideways. My heart and ego were bruised from years of disappointment and abuse. I was stuck on a perpetual carousel of pain and despair!

From the outside looking in, my life looked pretty good. What others could not see was that slowly, day by day, I was dying inside! I did not know what I wanted. I did not know which way to turn. I certainly did not know what I deserved or how to seek joy. The same questions looped in my mind day after day. "Is this as good as it gets? What am I doing with my life? What is my purpose? Do I even have a purpose? Does my life matter to anyone?" Regardless of how many times these tapes played, a glimmer of hope remained way down deep inside—you know, in that secret room of dreams, buried in the recesses of your mind—that maybe, just maybe…tomorrow would be brighter. With the dawning of each new day, I got out of bed and showed up for those I love, but secretly, I longed for the day to end. Have you ever felt that way?

I resigned myself to the belief some people are just born lucky, but others are destined to suffer—that I was destined to suffer. I convinced myself it was my plight to help others know joy at the expense of my own. That was how I lived for forty-six years—in silent suffrage. I knew deep down my viewpoint was pure bull, but having lost hope, it easily became a lie of more truth than fiction.

During the rare moments when I would find time to be alone with my thoughts, they would cry out, "There must be a better way to do life—some formula to build a better life."

I invested years and tens of thousands of dollars seeking the guidance of people who looked as if they had it all together, determined to figure out what they were doing right and what I was doing wrong. I believed if I adopted their ways and did what "they" were doing, then eventually my life would look like theirs.

I sought the help of counselors, therapists, doctors, and mentors. I attended seminars and read all the best motivational and self-help books. I invested in education and personal growth. I joined a gym, attended church regularly, chanted affirmations, engaged in visualization, and on and on and on. But nothing changed! Misery, pain, disappointment, and regrets continued to plague me. Perhaps, I was simply too broken or had experienced too much darkness for restoration—to know joy or love? There was one truth of which I was certain—my hope for a brighter tomorrow was growing more dim with each passing day.

In 2012, I hung a sign outside my house that said Purgioia Images (pronounced "Pure-joy-a"). I believed that by pursuing this newly discovered passion to become a professional portrait photographer, that I could literally, focus on the beauty within others. I guess I had this idea that if I could see enough beauty in other people, then maybe the ugliness of those in my own life, would fade away. Capturing animals, landscapes, and portraits brought me immense happiness. As long as I had a camera in front of me, I could turn a blind eye to the ugliness all around me. An added bonus was seeing the joy my work brought to others. Photography provided a way to escape the sorrows that haunted my spirit. I had no idea when I began my photography career, it would lead to discovering the formula I'd been searching for.

As a high school senior portrait specialist, I spent hours getting to know my clients. I planned elaborate themed shoots specifically around who they had been, who they currently were, and who they hoped to be. While I interviewed my senior clients, their parents would inevitably interject "the right" answer for their child.

After a few dozen interviews, I began to realize most of these parents did not know their kids quite as well as they thought they did. However, the biggest shock for me was that these amazing seniors had no clue—they were lost! I do not mean they were dumb or lacked common sense—actually quite the opposite. My seniors were the best of the best. They were beautiful, creative, talented athletes, overachievers, and accomplished scholars. They were driven, passionate, kind, and wonderful human beings with strong families. These were the kids doing life right! So why then were they suffering with anxiety, depression, uncertainty, low self-worth, and lacking in confidence? Why were they not more excited about the horizon just ahead of them? Have you wondered this of yourself or your own children?

I could not wrap my mind around why these incredible young people with résumés that put some seasoned adults to shame were lost. What they did not have a clue about was their value, their immense worth, and their awesome gifts and talents, let alone a tangible vision for their immediate future. They had no idea how to navigate the road ahead of them, and most were not receptive to hearing the wisdom of their parents. Most of my senior clients felt as if they did not have a voice in the creation of their story. That was a notion that overwhelmingly resonated with me.

I was most known in my portrait work for pushing boundaries that challenged my clients to step *way* out of their comfort zones. This meant coming face-to-face with many of their deepest fears and insecurities.

I intentionally would position my seniors in unstable, uncomfortable, and unexpected places while their parents looked on with a bit of anxiety of their own! But there was a reason for my unconventional antics beyond that of an adrenaline-filled adventure; I needed to break them down—to bust through their insecurities and gain their trust. I wanted my clients to walk away from their session with something far more valuable than a portrait. I wanted to play a small part in changing their trajectory from unfulfilled to joy-filled. I wanted them to see themselves through my eyes and the eyes of those who loved them. I wanted these kids to claim their worth and value!

I used their senior session to impart a granule of the wisdom I had earned the hard way, hoping it would encourage them to head true north. My desire was to show them they could face and overcome their fears and most importantly be confident and trust their instincts. Before I asked my clients to take any risks—like climbing a decaying tree or the roof of a ruined building or posing in the middle of a busy street or store—I went ahead of them. It was my responsibility to test the security and stability of the environment. This allowed them (and me) to see everything would be okay; all they needed to do was make the decision to go or stay. I gave them the directive to choose the right course of action for them! Each of my seniors heard these words when it got really scary, "Think about what you want, assess the risk, decide if what you want is worth the cost and the consequence to have it. If it is, then go for it! If it is not, then don't!"

They needed for me to reveal what was possible for them—but also to hold the space for them to choose their path. If they agreed to go, I walked beside them as they found the way into position. I never allowed them to face their fears alone. My unconventional ways instantly established trust between us and broke down the barriers of fear. Inevitably, my courage became theirs.

They would walk away from their senior portrait session emotionally stronger, more confident, and a little less afraid than they were before we began! It was not only my seniors who grew emotionally though; the parents got a new perspective for their child's inner strength and courage and ability to overcome—often in ways they did not expect. The best part of my job was witnessing a mom or dad as tears of pride flooded their eyes, bringing with them a little more peace and hope their babies were ready to fly!

It was because of these sessions I came to the realization that regardless of how manicured our lives look, we are all struggling with something. Those "somethings" are the opportunities for you and me to dare 2b more…—to dare to overcome and bring our best lives to fruition. The self-limiting beliefs I held—that doubt, insecurity, fear, worry, anxiety, and overwhelm, were emotions reserved only for those who had experienced the lousy stuff—were repeatedly shattered. My kids, as I call them, were changing me! Their courage was becoming mine.

Once I got beyond the delusions that suffering was reserved for the lost, a lightbulb came on. My seniors taught me that identifying what you want is daunting and overwhelming but identifying all that you do not want is significantly more simple.

And there it was—the formula for which I had been searching!

The formula came in three parts. The first was to make a commitment to dare 2b more… The second was to establish foundational footers that could support a DARE 2B MORE…™ life.

The third was to stop living like an employee in my own story and take my place in the C-Suite where I belonged. It was time for me to dare 2b more…Non-Negotiably, Joy-filled! It was time for me to take my rightful place as the chief operating officer in the "business" of my life. Today, I refer to that business as InJOYou, Inc.™!

In December of 2015, I made the decision to assign value to my joy. Fueled with a fiery determination to custom design and build a life of sustainable joy, I walked away from a twenty-two-year abusive and miserable marriage, financial security, and most of my extended family. I closed the doors to the toxic people, places, and things that had held my joy hostage for more than forty years. When I unpacked the last box in our new home, I collapsed to the floor in a pool of tears. I was terrified, relieved, excited, brokenhearted, but mostly worn beyond fatigue. It was bone-crushing exhaustion. I needed to rest my heart, body, and soul to rediscover who I was and who I wanted to become. It took a full year to recover from forty years of emotional, physical, spiritual, and mental abuse. I didn't know it then, but I was embarking on what would turn out to be a four-year quest to create a blueprint for how to build a joy-filled life from the ground up. In 2019, I finished that quest. In completing my quest, a new passion emerged—a burning desire to teach, mentor, coach, and empower others to build their lives to maximize joy and minimize regrets.

I still enjoyed being a photographer but had come to realize that art and adventure were not what ignited my passions. It was not the act of creating photographs that I loved; it was being in a position to impact the lives of young people—to help them see themselves in the same light as their loved ones, and I did, if only for a few hours. Photography was the vehicle that allowed me to see what I was truly designed to do. I was meant to use my pain and the wisdom garnered to coach, mentor, and teach others.

I wish I could tell you that simply abandoning the toxic people, places, and things that haunted me and discovering my true mission allowed joy to flood into my life instantly, but that would be a lie. Not only did joy not flood my world, but pain followed me into my new life. I had changed my dwelling, a few of the players in my world, and I was doing things my way. So, why was I still burdened—plagued by the same thieves of joy as before? I was still putting out fires. I was still restless. I was still stuck. I was still existing, void of real joy! I was doing everything the "experts" suggested! What was I doing wrong?

On January 12, 2018, two years after I had flipped my life upside down in search of joy, I figured out the answer to that question.

You Are Never Ready

Ring! Ring! Ring! I glanced to see who was ringing my cell; I think my heart stopped for a moment. A quick glance at my ringing cell indicated my mom was calling. I stared at that phone debating my response: Do I answer it or just let it go to voice mail? Suddenly, time stood still, allowing me the space to conjure the possibilities of why I was seeing her name on my screen. I knew this call meant my life was about to change.

My mom never called me. In fact, other than an occasional text, she had all but stopped speaking to me years ago. My mind flashed across multiple scenarios before deciding to answer. I thought, *If I hear her voice, then my stepfather is dead. If I hear his voice, then my mom is dying.* I tried to brace myself. I had absolutely no idea how to feel nor what I was capable of feeling. Nearing a state of panic, hesitantly, I answered the call. "Hello!" The line fell silent for a moment. Then the words I was not prepared to hear echoed across the line, "Laura, your mother is dead. She died yesterday at the hospital."

I could not control the hysteria that engulfed every part of my soul. I could not breathe. I could not think or speak. The light in my office turned to darkness. Was this real? Was I dreaming? Did I hear him correctly? Why hadn't someone called me sooner? There was still so much left to say! A wave of uncontrollable crying rendered me unable to formulate a single word more.

Laura, get a grip. Get back in control! You need to be strong. After all, you have been expecting this call for years. You were prepared to accept this fate! These were the thoughts that took turns screaming out in my head. All at once, my thoughts blended together into white noise, like that heard only on an old-time TV when the station suddenly goes out, and static is all that remains. The blaring noise ceased long enough for a single thought to emerge, *I should have called her.*

Monday afternoon, just two days before, I felt an overwhelming sense of urgency to call my mother. As I mentioned earlier, we had not spoken other than an occasional text here or there for many years. Our relationship was clutched by pains so intense, the jaws of life could not have freed us from its grip. Our righteous indignation could not give way to love, let alone forgiveness.

Countless times across the years, I thought of calling her but always rejected the urge. It just hurt too much to constantly replay the old tapes with her. But this time was different. I felt compelled to call her; there was a hurt inside of me only my mother's voice could heal. I wanted to talk with her for a spell. I wanted to lay my pains at her feet and have her tell me everything was going to be okay. After all, weren't moms supposed to be the place where their children, young and old, could seek and find comfort in the storms? Heartbreakingly, ours was not that kind of relationship. I believe in that moment God provided an opportunity for me to speak with her one last time.

I dismissed the opportunity because the emotional baggage was simply too significant to unpack one more time. I had forgiven her a thousand times over for each and every one of her crimes of motherhood, but without fail, every time we talked it ended the same way—in bitterness and anger. I wish I had had the courage to call her. She died the next day.

I know when God is calling my heart to action; I have always known! Subsequently, it never fails that when I ignore his call, I regret it.

I wish I would have denied the negative power that haunted my emotions that day. Perhaps if I had, the right space would have existed to allow forgiveness and grace to be our final gift to one another.

At my mother's funeral service, it was abundantly clear my presence was anything but welcomed. Those in attendance—including my stepfamily, my sister's family, and my mother's friends—all viewed me as the wretched daughter who broke her mother's heart. They were wrong, for it was my mother who had broken mine. But now, what difference did it make! I no longer cared what light they chose to cast upon me.

I laid my head on my mother's lifeless body for what felt like an eternity, screaming and crying, "Why? Why couldn't you have loved me? What was so wrong with me? I am so sorry I did not call you!" I truly did not realize the magnitude of heartache that still lived in me until I saw her lying in that casket. I believed because I had lived without her for so long the sting of her death would have been eased. That was not the case. If anything, her death felt like my own.

With the service about to start, I turned from my mom's body only to be met with angry faces staring at me. To my right sat my aunt, cousins, and boyfriend—all of whom were equally denied a relationship with her. To my left sat my stepfather, two stepsisters, and their families. My real sister accompanied by her sixteen-year-old-daughter—whom I had never laid eyes on—were seated among them.

When I was three and my sister five, we were separated by divorce. We were raised without the other. She resurfaced in our mother's life during the time of my absence.

Not only was I dealing with the death of my mom, but also the carnage of the past that remained very much alive. Gazing out at the showcase of divisiveness, I had an undeniable realization for the gravity of rawness that existed in this room, a lifetime of pain that had nothing to do with my mother's death. As I looked into each of their eyes, I thought no other person in this room holds her history as I do. No one else could possibly understand what I was going through; yet there I stood, the enemy of them all.

Even though she had been married for thirty years, not even her husband could have understood the pain that lived in me because of her. Not a single individual in that room knew or shared a history with this woman they came to pay homage to as I had!

What was I supposed to do now? Every wound I believed to be healed was ripped wide open. My guts were fully exposed; there was no way to hide from the pain. How was I going to recover from this? How was I going to let her go? The agony raging inside of me literally suffocated each breath I tried to take. My mom died on January 10, 2018, at 1:55 a.m. As her coffin closed, mine opened, unpacking forty-five years of emotional baggage—baggage I fully believed and trusted I had dealt with. I was wrong.

A week after my mom's funeral, I still could not get myself together. Both of my parents were dead. All my grandparents had passed. Four of my five uncles had died, and countless more loved ones and friends had come and gone. Life felt more fleeting than it ever had before. My twenty-two-year marriage had ended; my eldest daughter was a heroin addict and currently in jail serving her most recent six-month sentence.

Both of my younger children were doing great and heading off to college in just a few months—a reality I both celebrated and dreaded. My career was anything but extraordinary. I was drowning in the conflicting emotions of my reality. My thoughts were consumed with death—that of my own death. I wanted the hurting to stop. I needed the hurting to stop. I needed to be alone with my pain.

Free Falling

I booked an immediate flight to Naples, Florida. An hour after I arrived, I collapsed in a pool of my own tears. When I woke up, I went out to dinner and then to the grocery store. As I wandered the aisles aimlessly with tears waterfalling down my cheeks, it occurred to me I had never been grocery shopping for only myself. It was so strange to realize this in the middle of my despair.

Food and I do not have a relationship, so the concept of buying food for only myself, was foreign. I loathe grocery shopping because it is just one more area of my life structured to please everyone except me.

Later that night, I sat on the balcony with a glass of wine, gazing across the water and chatting with Jesus! It seemed completely and utterly ridiculous that these simple benign tasks had allowed me a bit of joy in the midst of this overwhelming despair. How was something as mundane and ordinary as picking out groceries able to soothe the pain of my shattered heart? I was certain I was losing my mind! Really? Groceries were a source of joy?

The following morning, I grabbed my laptop and a cup of coffee and made my way out to the balcony. As I sipped my coffee and soaked up the morning sun, it occurred to me that this was the first time in my life, I'd been alone, completely alone, with only myself to consider. There was no one I had to see, no one waiting for me, and no one coming or going. There was only me. No joke! I was forty-five years old and had never experienced being alone, free to exist exactly as I chose.

I owned my time—talk about a foreign concept. I met with Jesus for a while, cried deeply, and began writing without inhibition or direction. I titled the document, *"The Happiness Drug."*

The writing of that short article served as a launchpad to creating InJOYou, Inc. I will share the article a bit later in the book, but for now, know the article led me to the conclusion a considerable part of my misery was attributed to a perpetual pursuit of happiness. The intrinsic desire to "just be happy" yielded an overabundance of pain for everyone in my world but especially for me. I was done with chasing happiness; I wanted joy. The problem was I did not have the slightest clue what that looked like or how to find it!

My mind drifted toward the things I dreamed of doing or experiencing but forfeited for the happiness of others. I tried to imagine how it would feel to throw caution to the wind and follow my heart's whimsical desires. It was time to regain control of my emotions by getting wildly out of control! (If you are an adrenaline enthusiast, that last sentence will make total sense to you.) To clear the fog of despair, I needed to be unnerved, entirely, and outrageously shaken from this all-consuming depression. I had to find something that could set me free from the chains of this suffocating grief before they choked the last bit of breath from my lungs.

For whom or what have you forfeited your joy? If you could experience a single day without boundaries or limitations, what would you do? Where would you go? Who would you see? What wrongs would you right? What regrets are stored away in the trunks of your heart? I asked myself those same questions.

I considered driving at a hundred miles an hour down an open road, screaming at the top of my lungs, running away for good, dancing the night away in a drunken stupor, or just sleeping for the next ten days. None of those options seemed viable or particularly good for my freedom or health.

Next, I thought of all the things still on my bucket list—the things I wanted to see and do but had not because someone or something always stood in the way. Then it hit me…skydiving!

I was going to take a massive leap of faith and jump out of a perfectly good airplane. I wanted to feel the kind of freedom that being in control, of being out of control, could generate! Immediately, I thought of all the people who would be angry at me for this—the list was long. I thought of how selfish I was being. What if something happened and I survived only to exist as a burden on my family? What if I orphaned my children? Would they ever forgive me? Suddenly, my excitement was replaced with guilt, shame, and resentment.

And the argument began… People have been successfully jumping out of airplanes for decades. It is a regulated activity. It would be bad for business if people crashed into the ground and died, so I assume the instructors and pilots do all they can to prevent those complications…right? Then I asked myself the same question I used to ask my high school senior portrait clients. Is this worth it? It was!

I made the appointment and drove an hour up to the airport. After I arrived, I watched the informational videos and took the training class. Before I knew what was happening, I was suited up and crouched down on the floor of a tiny Cessna. At five thousand feet, my instructor Carlos exuberantly teased, "Look down! We are halfway there!"

The lump in my throat extended all the way down to my feet. I thought to myself, *What in the hell was I thinking? There is no way I'm going to jump out of this plane!*

The ten-thousand-foot ceiling arrived all too quickly. Carlos was grinning from ear to ear. I, on the other hand, was paralyzed by fear. It was going to take an act of *God* to get me out of this plane!

What happened over the next three or four minutes was more profound than anything I could have ever possibly imagined!

Faith has always played a role in my life, but until that moment, I wasn't able to fully communicate to others what having faith really meant; I'm not entirely sure that I fully understood. I got the gist, but deep down, I was not all in. Of course, I did not know this at the time, but it would not take long for that truth to come to light.

The fear of possibly orphaning my children made the climb to ten thousand feet anything but pleasurable. I was overwhelmed with hesitation and doubt. (Kind of like when we doubt in God or his promises.)

Despite my love for flying, looking down from ten thousand feet, knowing that I was about to exit the safety of the cockpit on purpose, transformed that love to paralyzing fear. Carlos, on the other hand, showed not even a hint of anything beyond exuberance. He grinned at me with a smile that I could not fathom in light of what we were about to do and said, "It's about that time! Let's get tethered." He instructed me to turn around and rest on my knees.

Ironically, on my knees was precisely the place where I wanted to be. (How many of us wait for that life-or-death moment before we drop to our knees, seeking God's attention?) As Carlos tethered us, I muttered, "I'm sure you hear this a lot, but you do get that I am putting my life in your hands…right?" I quite literally just put my life in the hands of a total stranger. (It is with blind trust we give our lives over to the care of Jesus, fully trusting in him with the outcomes.) Because I was tethered facing away from him, realistically, I could not verify that Carlos had secured me to him. For all I knew, he might be planning for us to plummet into certain death. (This is like the battle for control that we engage when God tells us to do something—puts a call on our heart—that requires us to give up our power and put our faith, hope, and trust in him alone.)

Carlos's reply caught me off guard. He said, "I need you to know that I am placing my life in your hands, too. If you panic or don't do as I instruct you, your actions will put my life in jeopardy." We were both blindly trusting each other with our lives, quite literally. Carlos was the only one who knew how to return us safely to the ground; I had no other choice than to trust him if I wanted to experience skydiving. I had to trust he was for my good! (Faith is being confident in that which you cannot see. God tells us countless times over, "Be courageous! Do not be afraid! I am with you. I will never leave you or forsake you.") Carlos flung open the cockpit door! The sudden gush and sheer force of the wind stole the air from my lungs but also, it freed me from the clutch of fear. Suddenly, I was fully present in a way I'd never before experienced; I felt calm—almost void of emotion. Faith was the only emotion I felt. (This is the clarity of mind we need to have when we approach God with our prayers. *Jeremiah 29:13: "You will seek Me and Find Me when you search for Me with all your heart."*) Placing his hand ever so gently on my forehead, Carlos whispered in my ear, "Are you ready?" I never spoke a word in response. I simply released the death grip I had on the cockpit dashboard handle, and together, we rolled out in free fall, ten thousand feet above the ground. (God tells us to give our struggles to him in faith. Trusting in God requires taking a leap of faith and saying "Yes" to his call, obediently and confidently.) A microsecond after we rolled out, I was overtaken with emotion. The emotions that encapsulated my being were not those of fear, anxiety, pain, worry, or hurt. No…they were those of peace, freedom, and pure joy—more pure and real than anything I dreamed joy could be! (This is the kind of freedom that comes when you truly, truly surrender control of your life over to the care of God, with faith and trust that he is working out all things for good.) It was everything and nothing I could have imagined all at once. Perfection is the only word to describe it! The world was still, balanced, and quiet, free of all pain, and incredibly beautiful. (God promises to each of his children an eternity that feels and looks just like that.)

Everything was in perfect harmony! Although I was void of control over my life—fully trusting my earthly existence to a man whom I'd never laid eyes on before now—while in free fall at 120 mph and doomed to death should anything go wrong—the thought of dying never once crossed my mind. I experienced a safety and freedom indescribable with words. (Jesus tells us that if we seek a relationship with him, trust him with our lives, place our faith in him, and remain focused on glorifying him, we will realize truth, peace, love, freedom, and sustainable joy…both now and eternally.)

When we landed, I finally understood what it meant to be faith-filled, to genuinely trust Jesus with my life. I understood the value and felt the rewards of faithful obedience. Because of that jump, I came fully to understand God is not only my Heavenly Father but also my best friend. I felt assurance that I did not need to be afraid; everything was going to be okay.

The sorrow consuming my heart, mind, and soul only an hour before was strangely just lifted; in its place, a sense of calm and peace I'd never known. I was still grieving, of course, but I was not suffocating anymore! I felt freed from forty-five years of existing in the shadows of despair. For perhaps the first time, I felt genuinely and completely alive.

I looked up at the sky and knew everything was going to be okay—I was going to be okay. I also knew I was done with hanging a "for sale sign" on my joy! I wanted whatever days remained in my life account to realize the same empowering and indescribable peace and joy I felt the moment we tumbled into freefall. From that moment forth, I made a commitment that I would honor God with my life and never again trade joy for happiness. I was determined to live out my days on purpose (to bring joy to God) and with purpose (to leave a legacy of joy for all those I would, someday, leave behind).

    I returned home and got to work! I opened a toolbox filled with priceless tools I'd collected over forty-five years and set out to build the "business" of my life to manufacture and distribute a product of joy! But first, I needed a blueprint!

Shop our online gift store @ www.Injoyou.com for motivational products like journals, tumblers, t-shirts, hoodies, shoes, and more. These products are designed to encourage and support you as you DARE 2B MORE… JOY-FILLED!

CHAPTER 1

Unfulfilled to Joy-Filled
A Love Letter to You

Family is a word that has taken on countless shapes throughout my life. Although my family included many, only a few were permitted influence throughout my childhood. The reasons for this are best summed up in the old saying, "Oh, what a tangled web we weave when first we practice to deceive." My family members included the usual players—Mom, Dad, sister, grandparents, aunts, uncles, and cousins. Most deemed forbidden fruit—unworthy or deserving of inclusion within our exclusive circle—a circle comprised of only my maternal grandparents, mother, her husband, his children, and myself. My father, sister, paternal grandparents, and countless others had their rights of inclusion revoked, denied, or limited. Eventually, these people with whom I shared the same blood faded into little more than a figment of my imagination. As I was growing up, a few of my exiled family members would resurface but for reasons I never fully understood, they'd vanish from *my life again*! I grew up feeling abandoned and unworthy of love.

Our tiny village was headed by my grandfather—the patriarch of our family. He set the standard for each of us and we believed his word to be the only, and final word of truth and goodness. He was truly, my hero! It was not until I learned of his crimes that I finally came to the understanding he was really more like a cult leader, hell-bent on creating an impenetrable fortress around the five of us, ensuring his crimes would go undiscovered! I was thirty-four when the light finally illuminated the truth that had remained in the shadows for three generations.

My grandfather was a child molester; he preyed on his own family, including my aunt, cousin, and my own daughter. But before he became my archenemy, he was my greatest hero! I adored him and believed him to be an angel on earth. He set the bar for all that was right and wrong and good and evil! My grandfather was the only person I trusted; his word was gospel! I was not the only one who believed he was our true due north compass—we all did! He was perfect; the rest of us were just sinners of a different flavor trying to win his favor!

My grandmother, mother, and I lived to make him happy. We would instruct anyone—husbands, boyfriends, friends—we brought home what behaviors were allowed and which absolutely were not. If anyone stood in opposition of our patriarch, he or she stood in opposition of us all, and therefore, was exiled. Looking back now, I clearly see how toxic he was, but for most of my journey, my entire self-worth was dependent on who my grandfather perceived me to be!

By the time I was fourteen, I had witnessed firsthand the enormity of evil that existed in the world while seeing little that was good. My childhood was tumultuous at best. The memories I have to this day are pain, loss, addiction, control, and an endless supply of abuse—emotionally, mentally, physically, and spiritually! My mind found a way to protect me from those pains by allowing me the grace to block out most of my childhood, except for those moments of impact that changed my trajectory and who I was meant to be.

When I was a child, my mother forced me to write letters to my grandfather. I didn't particularly appreciate doing so. Letter writing was, in part, to punish me for being inconsiderate and ungrateful in his eyes. When he wrote or called, he felt that my response—my enthusiasm—lacked sufficient appreciation for his generosity. Letter writing was meant as a corrective action to prove my love and devotion to him. The problem was, he repeatedly told me that I was "ignorant" and "too incompetent" to pen a proper "thank-you" letter. I honestly dreaded that chore; truthfully, I hated it because of what he did to my letters!

Mom would force me to sit at the kitchen table and pen a full-page letter to my grandfather once a week. I tried my best to be perfect, not forget a single comma or period, or misspell even a single word. The signature was equally critical to having penned a proper letter. After we mailed the letter, I would wait, filled with great anxiety, for my grandfather's response. He marked up my letters with a red pen, mailed them back, and for added measure and torture, initiated a follow-up call to confirm his assessment of my intellectual deficits and incompetence. I remember this one-time I wrote, "Hi, Grandaddy! How are you? I hope you are doing well." When I got my paper back, the word *grandaddy* was circled in red ink with a note that said, it is spelled "GRANDDADDY" (you should know how to accurately spell my name). Next, he had circled the word *well* and attached a note; *well* refers to a state of health, not a state of being. The proper word is *good*! To this day, I still pause to consider which is correct. I secretly worry that the one I am addressing may conclude I lack intelligence should I choose the wrong one.

My grandfather was my teacher in many things from learning to sail to conquering algebra. The endless hours of "instruction" left me feeling I was not enough. Because I loved him so much and his validation meant everything to me, I learned to strive for perfection. I also mastered beating the hell out of myself when I failed to obtain it. In many ways, that worldview did make me better, but it also solidified no matter what I did, regardless of my effort, I would never be enough! Nonetheless, I kept trying to win his approval until one day, when he pushed me too far.

I was fourteen, angry, and fed up with trying! I was living in Virginia with my mom and the third of my stepfathers (six marriages to four different men). Mom and I were in yet another fight resulting from yet another horrible thing I had done to evoke her anger. (I went to a bonfire at the beach with my friends.) Screaming she was fed up with me, she called my grandfather to come over.

He came over and walked into my bedroom; I was sitting on the floor at the time. He bent onto one knee, leaned downed, pointed his finger in my face, and with an intense scowl said, "Laura, I have seen the darkness of your soul, and it is ugly." I do not recall a single other word he spoke that day. With those words, my fate was sealed. In that moment, I became the person he just defined me to be! I no longer cared about anything, and the next two years of my life proved it!

I am writing this book as a kind of love letter to you! If you are reading this, then chances are pretty good somewhere along the line you have had a person or persons who showed up and made you believe a lie that changed you—caused you to pivot toward creating an unfulfilled life, guided by beliefs that you are not enough, unworthy, or incapable of building a life that is sustained by love, peace, and joy. There is only one reason I decided to write this book—despite being told my entire life that writing was not my forte. You! Yes, you, the person holding this book. Your pain and joy matter to me! If my stories and those of others, combined with the lessons and tools I've garnered over four decades, can disrupt your self-sabotaging dialogues, self-limiting beliefs, and the building of more regrets than joy, then my struggles and vulnerabilities are worth the cost. I hope to empower you to change your trajectory from unfulfilled to joy-filled!

I want you to wake up knowing you are enough and believing that you were created to experience a joy-filled life. It does not matter where you have come from or what your current circumstances are; you can pivot right now. Everything that has ever happened to you happened yesterday, an hour ago, a minute ago. It is in the past. Your past does not have to define your present or future.

I wish I could tell you change is easy. It is not! I wish I could tell you reading this one book will make everything perfect. It will not!

But what I can promise you—with my own life as proof—is if you are willing to use the tools I am going to equip you with, your life will change for the better, not just today but every day God allows you to have!

The greatest obstacle you will ever face in changing your trajectory from unfulfilled to joy-filled is unfortunately, and fortunately, yourself. Nothing of value will ever come without a cost!

Nothing of value will ever come without your sweat equity! Nothing of value will come by taking the easy way out. If you want to hold joy, to know joy, to realize a joy-filled life, you are going to have to earn it. You must make the choice to command it from this moment forward!

You literally have the power to custom design your life to manufacture and distribute a product of joy starting right now, right here, in this very moment! I can guide and equip you with tools, but at the end of the day, it is up to you to do the work! I can support your journey, but I cannot travel it for you!

So…let me ask you, do you want to live sustained by joy? Do you want to create a life that yields little regret? Do you want to get off the carousel of anxiety, pain, regret, and unfulfillment? Do you want to change your trajectory from unfulfilled to joy-filled?

If your answer is *yes*, then I am so excited for you, and I am grateful you have made the choice to allow me to be your mentor, coach, and tour guide in building your most joyous life!

I am going to challenge you to build a dare 2b more…life, one that can sustain the joy you most want. It will not always be easy, but that is okay because living without joy is not easy either! Do not quit! You are worth it! You deserve to claim joy as your own!

A dare 2b more…life is one of balance, honor, accountability, harmony, and intention. A life like that requires a strong support system. That is why your foundation must be supported by impenetrable foundational footers!

In case you are not familiar with that term, *foundational footers* is a term used in construction.

"Footings are an important part of foundation. They are typically made of concrete with rebar reinforcement that has been poured into an excavated trench. The purpose of footings is to support the foundation and prevent settling. Footings are especially important in areas with troublesome soils" (https://www.messerlyconcrete.com/footings—foundations.html).

Why in the world would I be teaching you about construction and foundational footers when I just said this book was about teaching you how to build a joyous life? I am pleased you asked!

The first step to building a life of joy is to change your perspective. Sometimes all it takes to see the rainbow is to change where you are standing! Most of us are taught life is made up of two compartments, work and family with our career or *job* being the primary focal point. We answer the question, "What do you do?" by communicating our *job* title, which may be that of an employee, manager, executive, or owner. This creates two problems. The first is that by stating your job title alone, you are validating a misguided notion that your entire life consists only of your job—that it takes precedence over everything else.

The second problem is that by defining the sum of who you are with your job title, you inadvertently become an employee in the "business of your life" rather than that of the chief operating officer. This is where I want you to make a pivot in your mindset.

Your life is the most important business you will ever run. *Stop* running it as if you were not the owner. You are not an employee in your story so *stop* acting like you are! You were created to be the chief operating officer for the "business of your life," as I have trademarked, InJOYou (Enjoy you and your life). Every person, place, and thing you invite into InJOYou is a partner or investor. Your partners have one job: to help you grow, sustain, and scale InJOYou, Inc. The vision of InJOYou, Inc., is to live and leave a legacy of joy. The mission is to manufacture and distribute a product of joy!

You are not an employee! Change your perspective! My intention is to equip you with the most important tools I have in my toolbox—the seven foundational footers that will most help you to support, sustain, and grow your joy. Although they are only one part of the complete master course I offer for how to intentionally dream, design, and build the business of your life, that of InJOYou Inc. to maximize joy and minimize regrets, this book is dedicated mostly to the seven foundational footers. The fact of the matter is, if you don't do anything beyond the work to pour these footers, your life and your joy will exponentially grow. I would love for you to experience fully, the entire Eco-Print process, but my hope is that at the very least, you will give yourself the gift of more joy by pouring these footers. (You can find more information about my master course at www.InJOYou.com)

Before we can fully dive into the tools needed to support the foundation of InJOYou, Inc., we need to distinguish the difference between joy and happiness. Do not fool yourself; they are not the same, however, both are ultimately what people want most. Happiness and joy are the reason we do everything we do! Even the drug addict, lying in the gutter, is injecting poison into their veins for one reason: to escape pain with the hope of feeling happy! Your perspective will determine how happiness and joy look from your vantage point! Perhaps, happiness is the very drug preventing you from building a joy-filled life!

THE HAPPINESS DRUG!

(Authored by Laura Williams, January 18, 2018)

What do you want?
"I want to be happy!"
Why do you want to be happy?
"Everyone wants to be happy!"
What happens if you cannot be happy?
"I will be unhappy!"
Why do you want to be happy *now*?
"Because I want, what I want, when I want it…provided the sweat equity is minimal!"

Sleepwalking, treadmills, excuses, bad relationships, unhappiness, desperation, lacking energy, longing for more… What do these words have in common? About 67% of the population! The Harris Poll, which has been conducting a happiness survey for the last nine years, surveyed 2,202 Americans ages eighteen and older in May 2017. The poll found only 33% of Americans reported being "Happy!" I am betting right about now you are thinking one of three things, "I am happy!" "I wish I were happy!" or "What is there to be happy about?"

I was curious what a Google search would return when the words "I want to be happy" were searched. Not surprisingly, a whopping 457,000,000 hits were returned as of this writing. I thought, *Hmmm…What if I googled "I want to be unhappy"?*

I was shocked to see 30,000,000 hits were returned. Lastly, I googled, "I want to be loved!" I thought this would yield huge results, but it only returned a mere 190,000,000 hits.

Searching the word *happy*, you will find around 3,870,000,000 results. Search the word *sad* and four times fewer results appear with the first "pro-sadness" link not appearing until page five. So, what is my point? People all over the world are asking Google how to find and capture "happiness"! What makes people feel such confidence that a Google search will reveal an antidote for unhappiness?

Albert Einstein said, "If you want to live a happy life, tie it to a goal, not to people or objects." An eighty-year study out of Harvard found the people who cited having happy relationships lived longer, more healthy lives. Everywhere you look, someone is promising a quick fix to overcome unhappiness.

Why do we feel or think or assume the gifts, talents, and relationships we currently have are mediocre or less than happy in the first place? How is happiness quantified, and who determined the baseline? What do we have to have or do or be to think ourselves happy? These were a few of the questions that kept coming up for me and eventually led to my rogue theory happiness is little more than a powerfully addictive drug suffocating joy from our lives.

Imagine with me for a moment—a toddler. Talk with him and play or cuddle with him, and he is "happy." Give a toddler a toy, and he is generally happy. Give him snacks and he is happy. Give him a play date and again, he is happy. But what happens when you take all those things away? You are left with a crying child, who is demanding you return those things to restore his happiness. Are adults really any different?

Happiness is fleeting; it is temporary. Once you have the very thing or person or object you believed would make you "happy," something else shows up and redirects your attention. Shiny things stimulate your senses leading you to feel if only you could acquire that other shiny thing, you would be even happier. Happiness is an illusion that truly is rather elusive.

The state of being happy is dependent on the fact that your circumstances have reached an ideal baseline. That baseline is different for every single person. This causes what I call the competitive comparison—the chase to acquire the something better that someone else has in pursuit of your happiness. Now this is not to say you cannot feel "happy" when things are not in perfect order, but it is to say happiness does not have clearly defined borders. It is not something anyone can reach or crossover into. Just like cocaine, heroin, or any other drug, it takes more and more "stuff" to arrive at the same level of happiness you previously had. What makes happiness vastly more different than joy is that when the storms of life roll in, that same "stuff" that brought you happiness quickly becomes irrelevant. Consider the family whose worldly possessions were lost in a storm. They are unhappy to have lost the things yet filled with joy to be alive and together. In the storms, joy is sustainable; happiness is not!

Happiness requires your focus be inward. What do I want? What do I need? What is in it for me? How can this person, place, or thing serve me? This mindset forces you to be in constant pursuit of the people, places, and things that best serve you. Happiness is something you chase and acquire. It demands you be in constant forward motion, which prevents you from being fully present in this moment.

Joy is reciprocal; it comes to you only after giving it away. It can't be bought or sold or possessed because joy is a choice that one makes, minute by minute, hour by hour, day by day, year by year! It is a state of mind, body, and soul. To find joy, you must travel to the intersection of love, forgiveness, gratitude, selflessness, humility, and faith. By giving to others from your personal accounts of time, treasure, and talent, dividends of joy will be returned to you, creating a surplus of joy in your overall emotional bank account.

Joy-filled people have these qualities in common: hope, faith, appreciation, gratitude, and they are abundant givers. Whether in plenty or want, a joy-filled person finds the sweetness in what already is—they don't waste their time or energy mourning or coveting what is not. Joy-filled people recognize that by sowing seeds of joy for God and others, they will inevitably reap an abundant harvest of joy for themselves. This is to say that you cannot give what you don't have. You cannot have what you are not willing to invest in. If a joy-filled life is what you truly want, then you have to start by making an investment of your time, treasure, and talent into the joy of others before yourself.

What comes to your mind when you hear the word *ecosystem*? Imagine for a moment a field blooming with glorious wildflowers. Birds and butterflies adorn the skies. Everything you gaze on for miles is glistening, backlit by immense color radiating from a newly formed rainbow after a spring shower. Children and adults are singing and dancing; all are jubilant!

Can you see it? Can you feel the warmth of the sunshine on your skin as you prance through the meadows of wildflowers? Can you feel the glee of those around you? It is like being in an ice cream store on a hot summer day. There is not much to fuss about. Imagine your soft smile billowing into laughter as your senses are overtaken by the pleasing stimulus surrounding you.

Now imagine that same sky fills with dark, ominous, cloud clusters—each casting intense lightning down to the earth. Thunder roars through the air. The winds are violently swirling. The birds quickly disappear, and the flowers are beaten down by hail. The people, who were just frolicking about in the meadows, instinctively run for cover. They are screaming in fear of being captured by the storm.

Let me ask you…Why in the world are the people running from the very place that just brought them so much happiness? What changed? Ahhh…Yes! Of course, the storm blew in and took all their happiness away!

This is exactly my point about happiness. It is not sustainable in the storms.

What if you could have a triangle of joy, peace, and contentment around you? Do you think the struggles and discomforts of life would still show up? Would anxiety, during times of uncertainty, still attempt to captivate your thoughts? Would there still be hours of darkness and grief or fear? Of course, but what would be different is the unshakeable contentment that resonates from deep within you, the contentment that only exists when faith and joy are the foundation on which your life's business is built—a foundation that includes a fully engaged support system, including the people, places, and things that feed your joy. They are your anchor when those dark clouds roll in and threaten to steal your joy. A spirit of joy evokes a sense of contentment that allows you to stay in place and ride out the storm, feeling secure and confident that this too shall pass. There is no fear or doubt that if you stand courageously for just a few moments more, what was once beautiful, will again be.

Faith, peace, and joy are intertwined. Happiness can exist without faith because it is circumstantial and tangible. Joy is neither and, therefore, requires faith to be sustainable. Where there is one, you will find the other.

Together they allow mankind to stand completely upright as the storms pass overhead in full confidence everything is going to be good again. Sustainable joy needs faith!

DARE 2B MORE… InJOYou.com

48 | Laura Williams

Chapter 2

DARE 2B MORE...Living

And those the Lord has rescued will return. They will enter Zion with singing; everlasting joy will crown their heads. Gladness and joy will overtake them, and sorrow and sighing will flee away.
—Isaiah 35:10 (NIV)

Let your joy be in your journey—not in some distant goal.
—Tim Cook

A dare 2b more...life means making choices that are so intentional; your dreams have no other choice than to come to fruition.

Awe...the healing powers of the Caribbean! What my family needed was a cruise! Yup! A cruise will surely cure what ails us. It did not, but it was a great trip! My husband and I, accompanied by our two youngest children, shared a wonderful Christmas together, basking in the warm glow of the Caribbean. We laughed, played, loved, and appeared to be a happy family! My husband and I had gotten pretty good at faking the reflection of a happily married couple.

When we arrived home from what was a truly wonderful family vacation, waiting for us was a letter from my husband's ex-wife that sparked a blaze of raging anger. As my husband read through it, his anger grew exponentially. Things were about to get really bad, really quick! His ex-wife had written to uninvite us from their son's upcoming wedding shower.

A few days before leaving for our cruise, my husband took their two sons to a football game. During the late-night car ride back home, an alcohol-empowered argument ensued. I was aware of the argument, but I had no idea just how toxic it really was, although I should have known.

Alcohol has this uncanny way of unleashing a person's tongue to speak *truths* they likely would not have otherwise. My husband—who was heavily intoxicated—presented his true feelings about his future daughter-in-law to his son. The things he said did not sit well with his son or his ex-wife. She and my husband were not exactly members of one another's fan clubs to begin with. I knew my husband's intentions were to protect his son from marrying a woman he perceived to be in sheep's clothing, but delivery was never his strong suit. After several hours of listening to my husband and his ex-wife scream obscenities back and forth, I had had enough.

Feeling overwhelmed and exhausted, I decided the only thing that would help ease the pounding in my head was sleep. Sleep was not something I typically enjoyed before midnight, so crawling into bed at 6:30 p.m. was way out of character. The next day I woke up feeling rather poorly. By 1:00 p.m., I found myself in a fetal position on the doctor's examination table. (The doctor's office was a place only near death could make me go.) At 7:30 p.m., I drove myself to the ER. By 11:30 p.m., the ER chief had admitted me. It turns out my lungs were engulfed with pneumonia. (Legionnaires to be precise.) E-coli was ravaging my system, and I was dangerously anemic. I spent the next thirty days confined to a hospital bed. I could barely walk more than a step or two without help. I was in tremendous pain and could barely take a breath. I heard death whispering in my ear.

I simply was not getting any better.

One night my doctor entered my room, sat on the edge of the bed, and said, "Laura, you need a blood transfusion immediately."

I asked only one question, "What if…I do not want one?"

"This is serious. If you refuse, then you very well may die," she sternly stated.

This was a choice I needed to think about because, little did she know, I was more terrified of living than dying. Dying did not feel like such a bad option. I was forty-one, and my life had left me fully depleted of hope and void of joy in every corner, except one. It was the corner where my children lived. I thought of them and of their life without me, and I remembered the vow I made to them—to always protect them from harm. I did not want to live. That was real. But if only for them, I had to live, so I conceded.

Thirty days of lying in bed and ten more weeks of recovering at home in bed for a hyper-driven, overscheduled, deep-thinking person can be likened to caging a wild animal and then tempting it with a juicy steak every hour on the hour. This was the first time my mind was unable to will my body into action. I could not be the person I had always been—filling the hours with busy to overcome the pains. I was forced to come face-to-face with myself and the life I had created! Reflecting on each relationship, choice, and mistake I had ever made also created a space for depression to blossom. I was beginning to regret having denied myself a way out.

I was lost and numb to life. There was no joy left in my soul, and beyond that of being a mom, I did not know who I was. I did not even know what my favorite color was, or if I was even a genuinely nice person.

I was a facade, a fraud, an incomplete shell of a woman, who if not for my children, had little reason to exist. How had this life of mine become as good as it gets? Where did I go wrong? How could I change things now? I was too old and lacked the right pedigree. What about my children and our family? I swore I would never be like my mom dragging my kids through six marriages searching for happiness. I did not know how or when, but I did know there was no way I could continue in this empty shell of life even though I had built it, brick by brick. I was forty-two, and the only thing I had ever known was pain, abuse, abandon, betrayal, and addiction. In the midst of feeling overwhelmingly sorry for myself, one word popped into my thoughts—overcomer! Wait a minute…that's right!

For forty-two years, I had climbed out of valleys over and over and over again. If there was one thing I was particularly good at, it was taking the hard hits and getting back up with one question, "Is that all you have got?"

I did not have a plan to escape from what was, so I tried to fix it. I tried to talk with my husband for the millionth time about our problems and all that needed to be resolved with us. He blamed me for all the problems in our marriage, my eldest daughter's problems, and those of anyone else he could think of. My husband knew how to engage in verbal warfare better than just about anyone. He fought with words that cut deeply, "You are just like your mother, nothing…and you never will be." He reminded me constantly if not for him, I would be lying somewhere in a gutter. Strange thing was, despite his having never, not even once, rescued me from a gutter, I believed him; I believed without him, living in a gutter was my only alternative.

Over the next couple of months, I tried to be more like the person he told me I was supposed to be. The more I tried, the worse things got. Deep down, I knew—I had always known—I married the wrong man. I loved him; there was no denying that. But his love for me was toxic. Our relationship was toxic for both of us, but for our children, it was becoming catastrophic. Our son began to lash out at me and his younger sister. Our daughter began to isolate more and more and smiled less and less.

The kindest gift we could give to our family was one of honesty. We simply brought out the worst in each other. Our amazing children bore the weight of the collateral damage our marriage produced. Our marriage was changing who our children were meant to be. My dream and the illusion that kept me invested—that I could fight our way into being that white picket family—was dying.

The idea of letting go of twenty-two years was as devastating as it was liberating. I knew the emotional and mental cost of divorce, having survived all five of my mom's divorces by my thirteenth birthday. I was terrified the price for staying together had grown far more than the price for parting ways. It took eight more months to accept that my dream of keeping our family whole would never come to be. I had to face my worst fears—being alone, broke, and resented by my children—and finally walk away. It was time to set my joy free. It was time to dare 2b more…

Dare 2b more…living means you are done with settling for anything less than abundant joy. It means you are ready to stop living like an employee in your life and finally step into your executive level position as the chief operating officer. Further, you are ready to commit to getting comfortable with being uncomfortable in order to build and leave a legacy of joy for all whom your light touches.

Dare 2b more…living is dropping the excuses and negative narratives in exchange for taking up accountability to custom design the business of your life to manufacture and distribute a product of joy.

Dare 2b more…living is not about living from a place of self-centeredness or selfishness. It is about choosing to grow as a person each and every day, choosing to show up for others in your best light, and surrounding yourself with "partners"—the people, places, and things—that feed your joy.

There are behaviors that are toxic, self-destructive, and inhibiting of your best life. Selfishness is one such behavior. Dare 2b more…living is *not* living in a spirit of self-centeredness or in a mindset of "I want, therefore, I deserve." It is, however, being selflessly selfish. Are you wondering what in the world that means? Allow me to explain!

There are two forms of selfishness. There is the selfishness of taking and the selfishness of growing. The selfishness of taking is the form that says, "I want more, but I am not willing to put in the work to earn more, so I will settle for what I don't want or just 'take' what I do want."

Selfishness of taking gives no consideration to consequences or the feelings of others. It also does not demand that you honor or glorify your values. Selfish taking serves your desires alone. It does not provide a measure of care for any other. A truly selfish person is one that will always be more content in chasing happiness than in building a legacy of joy.

Selfishness for growth is very different. This kind of selfishness is protective of your mental, emotional, and physical well-being but *also* that of others whom your choices impact. For example: You have a friend or family member who constantly comes to you for handouts yet refuses to get a job or do anything to change his situation. Time and time again, you've rescued him from the fall out of his poor choices by investing your time, treasure, and talent. Each time you step in and rescue this person, he promises to change—to get his act together—yet continued disappointment and heartache are always at the end of that promise.

Generosity is one of your core values. Being a loving and supportive person feeds your joy, but lately, rescuing your wayward person leaves you feeling resentful, frustrated, and undervalued—as if you are doing nothing more than enabling the problem. Negative emotions are significant withdrawals from your emotional bank account; you make too many withdrawals, and before you know it, your *joy account* is fully depleted.

You cannot pour out from an empty cup! To continue caring for others might mean that sometimes, you will have to establish boundaries that others might perceive as selfish. (Side note: It is usually the people depleting our joy that label us as selfish for choosing to retreat from their toxic behavior.)

By making a decision to no longer rescue or enable toxic people—denying them your time, treasure, or talent—you are demonstrating a selfishness of growth. Making an intentional choice to grant yourself permission to release your joy from the grip of toxic people or situations is like arming the security system at InJOYou, Inc. (*the business of your life*). Part of your responsibility and accountability is to protect your business from outside influences poised to steal your joy. To be selfish (or in a better light, self-preserving) for the purpose of honoring your mental, emotional, and spiritual joy is healthy for you and all whom you desire to serve.

Ultimately, a dare 2b more…life is challenging yourself to dare to be better today than you were yesterday—to be fully accountable and intentional for how the choices you make impact your joy, and that of others.

Are you ready to DARE 2B MORE…?

Great! Let's build your business—InJOYou, Inc.—*the business of your life*!

DARE 2B MORE… InJOYou.com

CHAPTER 3

INJOYOU, INC.
THE "BUSINESS" OF YOUR LIFE

Being Confident of this, that he who began a good work in you will carry it on to completion until the day of Christ Jesus.
—Philippians 1:6 (NIV)

Nothing happens until the pain of remaining the same outweighs the pain of change.
—Arthur Burt

Imagine for a moment, your childhood. Think back to the time when you allowed your imagination to run wild and free and limitless. Where did your imagination take you in your childhood? Did you build empires, fight fires, blast off into space, heal the sick, invent the next greatest thing, prepare delicious meals, create inspiring art, build zoos, or become president? How many of your childhood dreams did you bring to fruition? How many did you dismiss as childhood fantasies? How many regrets live in that dusty old trunk of ideas, safely tucked away in the deepest and smallest place of your heart? What if you could stop filling that dusty old trunk with more regrets? What if you could intentionally design your life to minimize regrets? How would that feel? What would that look like? How would your life change for the better? Close your eyes for just a moment and imagine yourself living a beautiful life sustained by joy! What needs to change in your personal and professional life for that vision to become a reality? What are you willing to change to grow joy in your environment?

When I was a young girl, one of the ways my friends and I added to our allowance was to put up lemonade stands.

I recall this one day when I was out riding my bike around the neighborhood and stumbled upon one such stand. The stand consisted of a plain square card table, a pitcher of lemonade, Dixie cups, and a sign. There was nothing particularly special about this boy's stand, unless you count the look of pure boredom on his face.

Curious about the amount of loot he might be racking in with his little booming business, I couldn't help but spy on his operation—from a distance, of course! Unfortunately, it did not take long for me to sympathize with his boredom. Not a single person stopped by his stand. *Clearly, he is not a good businessman*, I thought. I hopped back on my bike and headed for home. The entire ride I was distracted by the visions of how much better *my* lemonade stand was going to be.

My intrinsic gifts were ignited. I dreamed of a fabulous lemonade stand that would blow away the competition! I burst into the house, "Mom, I have a great idea!"

She responded in her usual harsh way, "What is it, Laura? I'm busy!" (Yup…busy killing my dreams.) Already deflated, I did the best I could to maintain my enthusiasm as I shared my fabulous idea with her. "Mom, I want to set up a lemonade stand with a beautiful tablecloth and a vase filled with colorful wildflowers. I'll serve ice-cold, fresh-squeezed lemonade in a beautiful glass pitcher, and add slices of lemons…like they do on the TV commercials! I'll bake some homemade cookies so everyone can have a drink and a yummy snack. Then I'll make a fancy sign that says, 'You Deserve a Treat Today! Ice-Cold Lemonade and a Homemade Chocolate Chip Cookie for only $1.50.' Mom, that's $1.00 more than the boy down the street! I'm so excited to set it up! What do you think? Isn't this a great idea!" My mother, in her usual, deprecating manner, respond with "Don't be ridiculous, Laura! Stop daydreaming and get your head out the clouds. You can have a normal stand just like the other kids. Go do something other than bother me."

I was far too young then to fully comprehend how my mom's harsh and belittling words were slowly eroding away at the person I was meant to be. Her words resulted in my dreams being crushed, and my excitement diminished for the possibilities that my gifts and talents might yield.

My mother's ability to crush my dreams, to make me feel worthless and insignificant, remained my constant companion throughout my childhood, adolescence, and well into my adult life. Her words shaped how I perceived my value and consequently, what I perceived I could achieve in life. It should come as little surprise that children raised in toxic homes often fall prey to leading toxic lives. I was no exception. I let the negative and demeaning voices of those around me convince me that life was nothing more than something we just survived. How vastly different my future might have been, had I known then, that God intended for us to use the strengths and talents he breathed into us for joy—his, others, and ourselves! I often wonder who I might have become had a few less dream killers existed in my ecosystem.

There was a time when I held on to my pain as if it were a newborn baby. I was completely in love with my pain, although I certainly would not have admitted that to anyone, especially not myself. I blamed others for my dreams never coming true. I wish I would have known then we were not meant to be employees in our own stories. If I had, then the depth of my regrets might only be ankle deep. But instead, today my regrets mount to depths that if I were to free dive for an hour, I'm not sure I would reach the bottom.

Reactive vs. Responsive

A good portion of the insanity I endured was a direct consequence of the choices someone else made—those of my parents, family, courts, husband, children, and chosen friends. There was a truth I did not want to recognize nor fully grasped until late in my adult years. There was a level of accountability that belonged to me in creating the life I had experienced. I was accountable for the choices I made regarding who I did life with and how my story was being written. When I started accepting accountability for the role I played in the creation of my circumstances, I discovered I had the power to stop living reactively and start living in response.

Reactive people are like a firefighter. They live in a perpetual state of ready, their hearts concealed by forty pounds of gear; always at the ready to douse the next blaze. They are constantly scanning the landscape looking for signs of trouble, the next defeat, the next let down, the next crisis! Reactive people do not "think" the other shoe is falling; they know it is. That shoe is locked on target and heading straight for them. Without a doubt, that shoe will be covered in crap and purposed to break their heart. Reactive people preanticipate where the shrapnel will inevitably land when the crap-covered shoe hits the fan. They attempt to minimize the damage before it strikes. It is a matter of survival! I lived my life in firefighter mode for forty-two years. Let me tell you—that was not living; it was exhausting emotionally, mentally, spiritually, and physically. But the worst part of choosing to live in firefighter mode is the wonderful blessings you miss out on while waiting and searching for the next crisis.

Responsive people, on the other hand, live in constant gratitude—appreciating and enjoying the sweetness of each moment. (Remember Dorothea and Leroy's secret scrolls.)

They live with a spirit that is peaceful and free, almost as if floating in a hot-air balloon—rising above the noise so to only see the beauty around them. These people are the ones we firefighters long to be like. Responsive people dream in vivid color and direct their steps toward bringing their best lives to fruition. They see not only the potential for limitless opportunities but never forget to appreciate the moments they have right in front of them. When the inevitable problems of this life surface, they pause to assess the situation, consider all the possible outcomes—positive and negative—and then make "intentional choices" that will honor their values and will best feed the joy of others as well as their own. Responsive people are able to do this because they understand what keeps their ecosystem healthy and fruitful. (Think of the community around you as your ecosystem.) They know what their boundaries are, what they value, and the immensity of their worth. People who live in response to life seek the opportunities to dare 2b more…all the time! They perceive failure as little more than opportunities to be better.

Which are you, responsive or reactive? Your answer is important because it will determine the lens through which you view your world—either happening to you or for you.

If you believe life is happening to you, then you are living as an employee in the business of your life. You are living in firefighter mode—reactively!

If you believe life is happening for you, then you are someone who intentionally chooses to live responsively. You have accepted your executive level position as the chief operating officer in the business of your life.

The Business Viewpoint

Before becoming a professional photographer almost ten years ago, I was an employee engagement consultant. My business partner and I designed and taught training programs to help executive leadership teams engage their workforce. I loved this work because we were instrumental in changing the trajectory of the employees from unfulfilled to joy-filled.

Ours was a unique style. We genuinely believed that to have an engaged workforce, the CEO, in conjunction with the leadership team, had to intentionally "custom design" a corporate culture that would attract the right talent (people) and repel the wrong. In other words, we taught the leadership team how to create a workspace that would encourage and grow the values and behaviors they most desired—the ones that would allow the business to grow and flourish. Whenever we were hired to "fix" the employees, our first stop was always at the CEO's desk. We understood a truth that our clients typically did not want to hear, let alone accept; if the employee weren't engaged, then they weren't the problem—the CEO was! Why? Well…because it's the CEO who establishes the corporate culture!

The chief executive officer (CEO) is accountable for designing the corporate culture and establishing the values that will guide it. The corporate culture guides how a company behaves toward its managers, employees, vendors, and clients. The values and beliefs that guide the company are what will determine the quality of the corporate culture. If the people are a "hot mess," than they are because the culture allows negative behaviors to take root and grow. Likewise, if they are engaged and thriving, it's because the culture is designed to encourage and grow positive behaviors.

The bottom line is this, if you are a CEO who desires an engaged workforce—talent that is joy-filled rather than unfulfilled—then you better choose values that will ensure that is possible!

On the other hand, it is the chief operating officer's (COO) responsibility to bring that culture to fruition and ensure that it is sustainable. The COO is accountable for hiring the right talent, communicating the company values, and establishing clear boundaries for what behaviors are acceptable and which are not. The CEO puts the full weight of accountability on the COO!

Whether you know it or not, you are a COO. Right now, today, this very second you bear the full weight and accountability of bringing to fruition the corporate culture your CEO most desires. You are the COO for the most important business you will ever run—the business of your life—InJOYou, Inc.

I would like to help you reframe how you view this life you are living. Most of us compartmentalize our lives into two categories: work and play. But that is a very short-sided view. The reality is that our lives are comprised of more than two buckets labeled personal and professional. Instead, consider your life as a business—a business we will call, InJOYou Inc. It is comprised of eight unique divisions—those of faith, relationships, career, finances, health, passions, curiosity (knowledge), and creativity. The vision of InJOYou Inc. is to build, live, and leave a legacy of joy. The mission is to manufacture and distribute a product of joy for God, others, and yourself. Your gifts, talents, strengths, choices, values, and behaviors are tools that allow you to produce a product of joy, but also one of pain if you are not intentional in what you choose to build. The people, places, and things that you invite into your business (into your life) are likened to your business partners. Your home, place of business and worship, community, and the environment surrounding each are likened to your investors that infuse a surplus of working capital into your business. These are the people, places, and things that support your lifestyle, add or subtract to your energy and joy, and support you in times of turmoil. Your current circumstances, including your relationships, career, finances, health, and legacy, are a direct reflection of how you have been running, or not running, your business.

Think of joy as a giant puzzle. When the puzzle is put together, your joy is complete and full. But if even one piece is missing, then your joy is incomplete. Keeping this in mind, imagine that each of the eight divisions of InJOYou Inc. is responsible for manufacturing one piece of the puzzle. When all eight produce their designated puzzle piece, InJOYou is complete and joy-filled. But if even one division fails, then the other divisions have to work overtime to make up for the one faltering. As is true in any business, when one part of the company fails to perform, it creates stress for the other parts. Stress leads to resentments, breakdowns in communication, decreased productivity, and workplace toxicity. The only way to avoid breakdown is for the COO (i.e., YOU) to equip each division with the resources needed to optimize production.

In other words, if you truly want to build a life of sustainable joy, you have to give consistent quality time and attention to each division of your life.

Let me ask you a couple of questions. How well are you currently running InJOYou, Inc.? Are you the CEO, COO, or an employee? Is your business of InJOYou, Inc., producing a product of joy or pain? Is your business growing and thriving? Have you allowed "weeds" (negative or toxic people, places, or things) to grow? Are "weeds" overtaking the health and vitality of your business? If you don't know, then I invite you to show me your life, and I will show you the right answers.

I would like for you to go look in the mirror. Yes, right now! What do you see? Who do you see? Do you see the person you want to be or always believed you would? What do you feel or think as you gaze into that reflection staring back at you? Do you feel the way you desire to feel? What would you like to see? How would you like to feel when looking into your own eyes?

Now close your eyes; picture your present life. Allow yourself to consider all the different aspects that make you, you. Does the picture that comes up for you look the way you want it to look? Do you feel joy? Do you see, feel, or think "my life is better than I ever dreamed it could be"? Or do you find yourself shaking your head, wondering, "Is this as good as it gets? How did I get here?" If the latter is you, then please know I understand where you are. The answer to your question is: *no*! This is not as good as it gets, unless of course, you choose it to be! You have the power within you to change your trajectory from unfulfilled to joy-filled!

I want you to take a few moments to imagine the business of your life, InJOYou, Inc. Keeping in mind that you have built it into whatever it looks like today. Everything, including the exterior, interior, decor, partners (the people places and things that you do life with), and your products and services are a direct reflection of the values you hold most dear. What is your corporate culture? How are your partners behaving toward you and one another?

Are your people excited to be there? Are you excited to have them there? What are they saying about you as they congregate around the water cooler? Now imagine your customers (i.e., the strangers who come into your life). What do they think of your business? How do they feel about the experience of interacting with InJOYou, Inc.? Are they smiling, laughing, and enjoying themselves, or do they look disengaged, frustrated, or like they are searching for the nearest exit? What kinds of people, places, things, and situations do you find are most attracted to your business? What do you want your partners to think, feel, and say about their experience at InJOYou, Inc.?

The picture you just imagined represents the corporate culture of InJOYou, Inc. Let me ask you again, what is the corporate culture of your current life? Does it look and feel as you once imagined? Are you living the life of joy that you were created and designed to know?

How are the conditions of your relationships? How do you feel about the condition of your career, health, finances, passions, or interests? Are you currently attracting people, places, behaviors, and things that increase your joy or only those that steal it? If you were to depart from this earth today, would you say that the legacy you have built to this point is the legacy you want it to be? Is it one of happiness and joy, indifference, or worse, one of disappointment and pain?

Building a successful business is not easy. There is a great deal of work and an endless stream of questions that must be answered before InJOYou, Inc., is prepared to manufacture and distribute a product of joy. Selecting the right leadership—the right CEO—is paramount to success. Your first executive action as the Founder of

InJOYou, Inc., is to appoint a chief executive officer (CEO). The CEO you select is the single most important decision you will ever make. Choose wisely! I bet I know who you think your CEO should be! You may be surprised to learn, it's not you!

DARE 2B MORE… InJOYou.com

68 | Laura Williams

Chapter 4

Leadership

Whoever dwells in the shelter of the Most High will rest in the shadow of the Almighty. I will say of the Lord, "He is my refuge and my fortress, my God, in whom I trust."
—Psalms 91:1–2 (NIV)

Leaders get out in front and stay there by raising the standards by which they judge themselves—and by which they are willing to be judged.
—Frederick W. Smith, CEO of FedEx

Who is your CEO? What legacy do you want to build? What products will you manufacture and distribute? How committed are you to success? What are your guiding values, both non-negotiable and flexible? What is your purpose, vision, and mission? Is your foundation strong enough to support your growth?

These are a few of the questions that you need to answer to run a successful business. I believe the most important place to start is by appointing the CEO of InJOYou, Inc.

What do you think of when you hear the names Southwest, Chick-Fil-A, Tom's, Home Depot, or FedEx? Don't certain values naturally come to mind? Great customer service, excellent customer experience, quality, transparency, leadership, and innovation are but a few words most would use when describing these companies. Why is that?

The leadership teams of these companies intentionally wove a clearly defined purpose, vision, mission, and guiding set of non-negotiable values into their corporate culture. They literally custom-designed a corporate environment, ecosystem, or culture (all interchangeable) that would only allow the behaviors and values they most desired to take root and grow. In other words, if an employee demonstrated values (behaviors) that were in opposition to exceptional customer service, superior quality, or integrity, their career at Southwest would be short-lived. SW's ecosystem is intentionally designed to weed out the employees whose intrinsic values are not in line with those defined by the company.

Southwest is what I would call a dare 2b more…company. The founders and subsequent leadership teams remain crystal clear about who they are, who they want to be, and what kind of company they refuse to be. All those who work for SW honor the way SW has decided they want to conduct business. Companies who dare 2b more…do not waver in their values. If you want to be a part of their team, you are accountable for adopting their corporate values, mission, and vision as your own, at least while at work.

What I have affectionately coined the "Eco-Plan" (my version of a business plan) was born out of these premises. Just as a business must be intentional in designing a corporate culture that will attract the right partners—the people, places, and things—you, too, must be intentional in custom designing the corporate culture of InJOYou, Inc. The people, places, and things you currently or have previously attracted are a direct reflection of your values and the choices you have made. In other words, what you send out, you will receive back.

The CEO is like a lighthouse; they are the beacon that guides the business. InJOYou, Inc. needs a CEO who is unwavering, dependable, trustworthy, and capable to direct a course that is fruitful and joy-filled. You are accountable for choosing the right CEO to lead InJOYou, Inc. There is a catch, and you may not like it! It cannot be you, at least not if a life of sustainable joy is really what you want! Right about now, I bet you are saying, "Hold up…Wait a minute. That is not right. I am definitely the CEO in the business of *my life*. No one is going to run my life but me!" Allow me to explain why you cannot, or should not be, the CEO of InJOYou, Inc.

To reiterate: The CEO decides what the purpose of a business is. The CEO's "purpose" will drive the company's direction and decisions. Anyone who works for the company is accountable to honor the values, vision, and mission of the CEO. The CEO also determines the "why" for the company's vision and mission. If the CEO changes directions, has a bad day, or becomes distracted, the purpose, mission, vision, and values often become unclear for everyone else. Every facet of the business is subject to the whims of the CEO. That can lead to a breakdown in the overall health and sustainability of the corporate culture, which will also deteriorate the quality of the products the company manufactures.

The COO (chief operating officer), on the other hand, is accountable to drive forth the CEO's purpose, direction, and values and to also ensure anyone associated with the business from employees to vendors and clients also honor them. The COO is ultimately accountable to the CEO. In other words, the COO has an authority greater than themselves to whom they are ultimately accountable.

If you are the CEO of InJOYou, Inc., then your purpose, decisions, directions, and values are not held accountable to a higher authority! That makes InJOYou, Inc. (the business of your life) vulnerable to deterioration or collapse! Why? Because when the buck stops with you, you can and will make up the rules as you go along! There is no one to "check" you!

Accountability is required if living a life sustained by joy is ultimately your desire. You may be wondering, "Well if not me, then who am I supposed to appoint as the CEO of InJOYou, Inc.?" I am so glad you asked! Ultimately, that is for you to decide, but I will share with you who my CEO is and why.

God is My CEO

God is my appointed CEO. I am ultimately accountable to him for my choices. The values God directs are the values that guide the business of my life and thus my choices. Unlike myself, God and scripture are unwavering, constant, concise, and consistent.

God's purpose for his children (the whole of mankind) is to live lives that honor and glorify him—to bring him joy. *("Everyone who is called by my name, who I created for my glory, whom I formed and made" [Isaiah 43:7, NIV].)* In exchange for appointing him as your CEO, he promises to guide you through the storms with peace and joy, and comfort and confidence. *("You make known to me the path of life: you will fill me with joy in your presence and with eternal pleasures at your right hand" [Psalms 16:11, NIV].)*

God gave us a pathway to become heirs to his kingdom—to know an eternal life of peace and joy. To acquire this awesome gift requires only that we believe in his Son, Jesus Christ! Imagine receiving eternal life in exchange for only your faith and trust in Jesus; it proves the enormity of love, grace, mercy, and forgiveness that God has for us. We each put our hope and trust in something; I choose the only *something* that offers a promise of eternal joy.

God is my CEO because I want both earthly and eternal joy! I want to live with peace in my heart. I need clear directives and values because I am weak in my flesh. I have proven again and again that my way does not lead to sustainable joy. It has been my experience when I try to do life without God, my path was filled with potholes, dead-ends, heartache, and an internal restlessness, which lead me into a perpetual state of chasing happiness to fill the voids.

As I stated at the onset, only you can decide who or what to appoint as CEO for your business of InJOYou, Inc. You may not know God. You may not want to know God. That is your prerogative and your choice. This is your journey! Your belief systems might be different from mine; that is okay.

I am not here to judge you; but to impart the wisdom I have garnered based on my own experiences. You may hold the belief that a higher power by a name other than God needs to be the CEO of your life's business. Again, that is entirely up to you!

Wherever you are right now, that is okay! The truth remains that your CEO needs to be infinite (substantially greater than yourself) and also be a source of true and lasting hope. Your CEO needs to be consistent in nature for your joy to be sustainable. Allow me to share an example that justifies my thinking.

Let us say you are of the mindset that your family or money should be your CEO—holding the top executive seat at InJOYou, Inc. That would mean that your purpose, vision, mission, and values are determined by your family or money. (Stay with me! Remember, the CEO determines the purpose and the guiding set of values for a business.) There are a couple of things to consider. First, no one has control over death (meaning a person cannot will or stop death from occurring either naturally or at the hand of man). Second, individually, you have zero control over the entirety of the economy. Your money is always at risk, regardless of plenty or want. In light of these truths, what happens to the stability of InJOYou, Inc. (your life's business) should you suddenly lose your family, job, or the ability to earn money? If either of these things were to happen, then suddenly InJOYou, Inc., is left without a CEO. What happens to the clarity or solvency of your values, purpose, vision, or mission if suddenly you lost the people, places, or things that you appointed to be the CEO of InJOYou, Inc.? There is a reason for the saying "money cannot buy happiness." It is because money buys "things." Things can only pay you a dividend of temporary happiness! Things will never pay you a dividend of joy! Don't believe me…

Think about the last thing you could not wait to purchase—that thing you just knew was going to make you so happy. Maybe it was a car, house, pool, new suit, a trip, or some cool new toy. Do you remember how you felt when you finally got your hands on that thing you greatly desired? I will bet it made you feel abundant happiness, optimism, and excitement. Now let me ask you: How long did it take for that euphoria to wear off? How long was it before that incredible, life-changing purchase found its way to the shelf because a better more exciting and newer shiny thing caught your attention? Things do not provide lasting joy! Things bring us temporary happiness. Happiness is circumstantial and fleeting! If you want joy, then you have to start by stopping—*stop* chasing happiness! Happiness will come and go, but joy lasts forever!

Ultimately, if you drill down long enough, the answer to the question "What do I want?" is "I just want to be happy." If you want to have a "happy life" (as opposed to happy moments), then *joy*—be it your own or God's—should be appointed as the CEO at InJOYou, Inc. The best C-suite seat for anyone who desires to build, live, and leave a legacy of joy is that of the COO (chief operating officer).

Your accountability as the COO is to scale InJOYou, Inc., so that in the end (when you depart this world) your business will leave a legacy of joy for others. The people, places, and things you invite into your "business" are the investors or partners who will support InJOYou, Inc., with manufacturing and distributing a product of joy.

A business needs working capital to grow and thrive. InJOYou, Inc., also needs working capital to scale. The choices you make are like investments. The better you invest, the greater surplus you will have in your emotional bank account. Make a few bad investments and your surplus will quickly become a deficit. You cannot give from an empty cup; InJOYou, Inc., needs a surplus of joy in the emotional bank accounts in order to manufacture and distribute a product of joy. Joy is reciprocal! When you give joy, you will, in return, receive dividends of joy. The more you give, the greater the surplus you will have in your emotional bank account!

Some people are dealt hands that reveal no kindness whatsoever, yet they take those struggles and unfairness and turn them into blessings for themselves and others. Let us not pretend life is easy for anyone. How many times have you sized up someone else's life and concluded, "Now there is a person who has it *'all'*?" It does not even register to you that perhaps they, too, have been dealt some hard blows. Maybe they have also experienced heartache and disappointment. Struggles with money, health, addiction, mental illness, depression, divorce, disappointments, and loss are not escaped by anyone, regardless of socioeconomic status. A surplus of money certainly makes life easier, but it will never spare anyone from experiencing the storms!

Here is the thing—you can spend your days and nights wrapped up in a blanket of struggle, feeling sorry for yourself, blaming your circumstances, or you can recognize that no matter how hard you think your life is or has been, there is *always* something you can do about it.

I can promise you it is your beliefs about your struggles, regardless of how enormous or minuscule, that keep you encapsulated by them. If you believe you have no control in your struggles, you have chosen to be an employee in the creation of your story. As an employee, you relinquish the title of COO, but worse, unwittingly you have promoted despair to serve as your CEO. Choosing to be an employee in your story is literally like choosing to rent "misery," the penthouse suite in your mind, on purpose! Additionally, by opting to be an employee, you also relinquish the right to have a say in the design, health, and longevity of InJOYou, Inc. STOP living uncomfortably, comfortable! *You* are not meant to be an employee! This is your life; step up and start running it like a Boss!

The minute you give your pain the power to paralyze your forward momentum, you give your power to the hardships you claim not to want. If there is breath in your body, a thought in your mind, or a desire in your heart, then you can dare to be more.

Dare 2b more…is choosing to be more kind, more thoughtful, more patient, more giving, more disciplined, more diligent, more accepting, more fearless, more adventurous, or a million other positive descriptors. We all have areas of our lives where we can show up in some better ways. People are intrinsically drawn to the path of least resistance. We are creatures of comfort and feel safe in what we know, even if what we know is miserable or self-destructive. We are wired to be cautious or fearful of the unknown. People are also intrinsically lazy in how they show up for God, others, and themselves.

I guarantee you there is a person, place, or thing where you hold back, give less of yourself, or grant excuses permission to stand in your way. It may be a promotion you want, but you are unwilling to learn a new skill set. It may be a project you keep putting off. It might be a date night you were too tired to have. It might be a pile of laundry you put off until tomorrow. It might be the addiction for which you refuse to seek treatment or the toxic relationship you will not grant yourself the courage to leave. Maybe the person you withhold the most from is you by believing the self-sabotaging lies you've convinced yourself are true.

Whatever "it" is, if there are behaviors, activities, people, or something else negatively impacting your joy, then you need to dare 2b more… Remember the people, places, and things you invite to share in your life are your partners at InJOYou, Inc. They should be partners who invest in your joy as much as you invest in theirs. If they aren't, then you are allowing them to steal from your emotional bank account.

Whether you take ownership of it or not, there is a part of your life where you have stopped showing up with your personal best. There is an area where you have become so comfortable you have stopped being an active participant in your story. Willingly, you have traded a position of authority for that of an employee of little power. Man, by nature and design, is consistently inconsistent. We are weak in our flesh—easily tempted by shiny things, fast money, and the easy way around.

This is precisely why you cannot be the CEO of InJOYou, Inc. Joy-filled people have clarity about who is writing their checks and precisely what they will earn. They appoint a CEO who guarantees dividends of joy. God is the only CEO who guarantees to compensate your work with emotional freedom, peace, love, and joy.

Who is your CEO? Is it you, family, fun, money, love, greed, ambition, laziness, victimization, pain? If it is something other than joy (hopefully God's joy), I must ask you, *why*? What is your profit or payoff for appointing anything other than joy as your CEO?

Everyone, no matter who you are or what status you have reached in life, answers to someone. Personally, I want the person who holds me accountable in death, to be the same person I hold myself accountable to in life.

Let us assume just for conversation's sake that I am wrong about the existence of *God*. (I am not, but again for conversation's sake.) First, let me ask you this question: What if you are wrong about God? Do you want to find out the moment your life is over that you were? Maybe you think, "Well, if God is real, then he is also as you say, forgiving and loving. I'm a decent person. He will understand why I denied him and let me in any way." (This is what I hear from agnostics and atheists all the time.) Imagine that you showed up to the Super Bowl, walked up to the coach, and said, "Hey, Coach, put me in. Trust me, I really can play even though I have never thrown a single pass nor caught a single ball." The coach will look at you and say, "I'm sorry, but I do not know you… No, I will not put you in." You will never earn a Super Bowl ring if you never step foot on a field. Second, would you agree that it is preferable to live your minutes, hours, days, and years joy-filled rather than pain-filled? Would you prefer those you love and cherish to stand by your graveside, whispering, "My life was full of joy and love and goodness because you were a part of it" or "You were a source of disappointment, pain, frustration, and sorrow"? Make no mistake about this, whether you are five, fifteen, or fifty, you are building a legacy right now. The people you interact with, share life with, work alongside of, or merely brush by are impacted by your choices, the way you treat them, how you show up in times of plenty and want, and by the words you speak and the actions you take. Remember Dorothea and Leroy from earlier on in this book? They were people I knew only a few hours, but they are the reason this book now exists! You never know how your life is shaping that of another! The measure by which you give is the measure by which you will receive! Give joy on purpose, with purpose, and it will be returned to you by a greater measure than you can possibly imagine!

My point is this: Whether you believe that at the end of your life, God will demand you give an account for how you spent the days he gave you or not, the truth remains, those you leave behind will render an accounting of the life you lived. The questions you need to answer are, Who am I ultimately accountable to? What if choosing God as my CEO is how I realize a joy-filled life of little regret? What legacy have I built to this point? Is it one I want to continue building? The question remains: What legacy do you want to leave for those that matter to you?

If your desire is to build, live, and leave a legacy of joy, then you have no other choice than to lead with values that create the space for joy to grow—values like kindness, compassion, love, work ethic, generosity, integrity, truth, and humility. The corporate culture of your life will decide the legacy you leave for all those who experienced life with you.

In Galatians 5, we are taught the fruit of the spirits are these: love, joy, peace, patience, kindness, goodness, faithfulness, gentleness, and self-control.

I choose God because not only are the values he dictates in line with the legacy I wish to leave, but God also grants forgiveness, a source of awesome hope, reminds me I am never alone, and has proven, at least to me, that his ways always turn out better than my own.

God is the CEO of my InJOYou, Inc.! Who or what will you appoint as the CEO of your InJOYou, Inc.?

DARE 2B MORE… InJOYou.com

Chapter 5

Ecosystem

Therefore, everyone who hears these words of mine and puts them into practice is like a wise man who built his house on the rock. 25 The rain came down, the streams rose, and the winds blew and beat against that house; yet it did not fall, because it had its foundation on the rock.
—Matthew 7:24–25 (NIV)

A business ecosystem is just like the natural ecosystem; first, needs to be understood, then, needs to be well planned, and also needs to be thoughtfully renewed as well.
—Pearl Zhu, Digital Maturity: Take a Journey of a Thousand Miles from Functioning to Delight

Imagine for a moment a blistering hot, dry, and sandy desert. Intense sunrays penetrate every inch of the land's surface. The land is barren, void of water, trees, and adequate food. Now imagine a swamp. The riverbanks are shaded by trees adorned with long strands of moss. The air is hot and rich with humidity. The swamp offers a bountiful feast of fish, birds, and reptiles. Visualize an alligator floating just below the surface of the murky river.

One day someone comes along and relocates the alligator. They take the alligator from the swamp that is abundant with the resources needed to sustain the alligator's life and relocate it in the desert. What do you think will happen to the alligator? Will it adapt and thrive?

Will it have food to hunt? Will it find water to cool its body? Of course not! The desert ecosystem is intentionally designed to ensure the alligator will not survive! The alligator will die. It is a certainty!

In Niagara Falls, on the Canadian side, is one of the most beautiful of butterfly conservatories I have ever visited. The inside is adorned with gorgeous green trees, cascading vines, and plants decorated by vividly colored blooms.

Before entering the habitat, visitors must pass through a powerful wind chamber. This ensures that no one who enters the habitat is also a host to anything that could disrupt the custom-designed ecosystem's balance. Guests are instructed, in no uncertain terms, not to touch the butterfly's wings at any time. It is acceptable for them to land on you, but you are not to touch their wings. The butterflies are so delicate the oils and bacteria from your hands can prevent them from taking flight.

Walking through the winding paths, you cannot help but to acknowledge the immense beauty and variety of each and every element of this ecosystem. Each of the elements exists in perfect harmony.

The temperature, humidity, soil, and plants were intentionally selected and incorporated for one reason, the butterfly's health and well-being. Before exiting, guests pass through another wind chamber, ensuring none of the butterflies have hitched a ride out of the enclosure on their clothing; they would likely not survive beyond the conservatory walls. Everything inside has been intentionally custom-designed for the health and well-being of these fragile and spectacular creatures. As a result of those intentions, over two thousand butterflies, comprised of forty-five different species, peacefully and organically cohabitate. The soil is the foundation for this sustainable ecosystem. It is what allows the right vegetation to grow. The right vegetation is crucial to the survival of every butterfly.

Despite the enormity of intention and care that went into building the perfect ecosystem, there are still elements that can threaten its survival. Mosquitoes can infect the butterflies with disease, nonnative fire ants will eat the butterfly eggs, and the life sustaining vegetation makes quite the feast for invasive caterpillars. These are invaders, likened to weeds—they suddenly show up, take root, and grow with extreme veracity, destroying the entire ecosystem's balance and harmony sooner than later. Weeds, if given free reign, can kill an entire ecosystem.

A huge factor in custom designing an ecosystem that can sustain the life you want is recognizing and labeling those partners—the people, places, and things—that are weeds. If you cannot identify them, they will come like a thief in the night and take root! Just as the desert ecosystem is designed to prevent the alligator from moving in, your ecosystem should prevent potential weeds from taking root. That can only happen when you intentionally design it from the soil up.

You and I, like the butterflies, require the right elements in our environment that can work together cohesively to support, grow, and ultimately, sustain the joy-filled life and lifestyle we most intrinsically desire.

The Ecosystem of InJOYou, Inc.

Have you ever stepped back and taken a peek through the proverbial window of your life? Have you ever thought I do not belong here? Why does it seem that I don't quite fit in with my village? Why am I different from those in my family? They do not understand me! Or…Are you kidding me? These just cannot be my people. Or…Why do I feel so discontent in my life? Maybe the questions that you ask are considerably less deep but equally as nagging. For example: Why am I always bored? Why do I feel so restless? Why can't I ever seem to get from point A to point B? Why is everything always so hard?

If not answered, these are the kind of questions that often lead to self-doubt, anxiety, low self-esteem, confusion, and even depression.

These are the kinds of questions that can cause you to feel as if there is something wrong with you, prompting you to morph into someone you were not created or designed to be. Your friends and family might attempt to validate you by saying something like, "You are just trying to find yourself! Keep trying you'll get there eventually! Do not worry about it, everything will work out. You are just going through something right now! It is not you; it is them." What "they" rarely say is, "You are right!"

Perhaps there is a good reason you have those nagging feelings that won't turn loose of your thoughts. It's entirely possible that you are trying to grow in an ecosystem that is not designed to support your growth, let alone sustain your joy.

What if your restlessness is a prompting from, as I believe, the good Lord above, urging you to move, to pivot, or to change the people, places, or things in your life that stand between you and the joy you most want?

To clarify, negative voices that cause you to feel small, demeaned, and devalued, or cause you to question your worth are not from God. Don't ever rent the negative voices of sabotage—your own or others—an inch of space in your mind. Negative people are like weeds in your ecosystem. If you allow their negativity to take root, that negativity will grow and eventually destroy the health of your entire ecosystem. Supportive partners are those who lift you up, encourage you, and genuinely care about your joy! Partners who are mentally, emotionally, and spiritually healthy for your ecosystem will speak truth into your life with compassion, respect, and encouragement.

A healthy ecosystem is comprised of all living and nonliving things—all things, both individually and collectively, working together to support, nurture, and inspire growth for all its parts, resulting in a balanced and peaceful environment.

Like an ecosystem, your life is comprised of living and nonliving elements. Each element either works together in harmony for your joy, or they work against each other creating discord. You live in an ecosystem. The real question is whether or not you've custom-designed it, were born into it, or accidentally stumbled across the border.

There are countless factors in your current ecosystem that either empower or deteriorate your ability to become the person you most want to be. These factors include habits, behaviors, people, places, and things. When the living and nonliving elements of your ecosystem work against each other, the result is an absence of balance or peace. When you lack balance, your spirit becomes unsettled; you feel a sense of restlessness, overwhelm, or anxiety. You feel as if you're pressing on the gas but stuck in neutral—going nowhere fast!

I would imagine right about now you're taking a mental walk through your ecosystem, curious if you've intentionally custom-designed it or are trying to grow where you were planted. Let me clear something up. There is a difference between "growing where you are planted" and custom designing an ecosystem. Growing where you are planted requires you to adapt to another's ecosystem, which may or may not support the life you want! Custom-designed ecosystems are a direct result of making intentional choices regarding the people, places, and things that are and are not allowed to grow and thrive in your environment. Who and what coexists in your environment do so because of your intentional choices! If you want to experience a life that maximizes joy and minimizes regrets, then it's time to custom design your ecosystem.

There are many reasons to custom design an ecosystem, but the greatest is sustainable joy. By defining and then immersing yourself in the right ecosystem—one that encourages, supports, and can nourish all eight divisions of InJOYou Inc.—your joy will exponentially grow and be sustainable when those unexpected storms blow in!

Are you wondering how exactly one goes about custom designing a joy-filled ecosystem? I'll be candid with you—it's a process that requires honesty, commitment, grit, patience, and faith! It requires you to dare 2b more…

Erecting a building occurs in phases, so does building InJOYou Inc. The first phase is known as "clearing the ground." During this phase, the moments of impact that changed your trajectory from joy-filled to unfulfilled are addressed and cleared. Phase two consists of pouring the foundational footers that will support the ecosystem you build. Phase two is critical to your success, which is why I am writing this book. Without a strong foundation, InJOYou Inc. is subject to erosion and collapse. Stage three guides you through a step-by-step process of designing a blueprint for your most joy-filled ecosystem. Stage four is all about the buildout! (You can learn more about phases one, three, and four, at www.InJOYou.com.)

Before you can custom design your ecosystem or attract the right partners to help you build it, you have to get reacquainted with your intrinsic self! Who are you? What do you value? Who and what grows and steals your joy? Depending on the life you have created to this point, these questions may feel overwhelming, daunting, or even exhausting.

People say this a lot, "I just feel stuck!" Often, they are not unhappy or existing in a dysfunctional life but rather hear a small quiet voice challenging them to move in other directions. "Stuck" does not always wake you with clanging bongs of misery, gloom, or doom, screaming, "Hey, buddy, your ecosystem needs some serious

CPR." It may be that "stuck" quietly wakes you each day with a burning question that seems to haunt you deep in the recesses of your mind. Is this it? Is this as good as it gets? What am I doing with my life? What is my purpose? These are the kinds of questions that lead us to the ultimate quest, a search for the single most important answer to the single most important question: What is my purpose?

The trouble with questions is they demand answers. When you do not provide them, the questions turn up the volume. Unanswered questions can get so loud that you will no longer be able to hear anything but the voice of doubt. Do not get me wrong. That little annoying voice of doubt sometimes serves as a measure of self-preservation to keep you from heading in the wrong direction, but it can also be like a nail in your tire, stopping you dead in your tracks, leaving you stuck. Doubt creates the excuses or weeds that inhibit your ability to cultivate a healthy ecosystem.

Questions are gifts, given to you by our creator, as I believe, God, to prompt you to dare 2b more…than you are or have been. There has never been a solution or invention created, which did not first start with a question.

What questions are coming up for you right now? Which of your questions are nothing more than doubt acting as a roadblock to prevent you from moving toward your dreams? What excuses have you accepted as truth? You cannot navigate the roadblocks if you refuse to accept they exist!

We are meant to live with a spirit of joy and peace. As the COO, you are accountable for building InJOYou, Inc., in an ecosystem that can best support its growth!

Let me ask you: if you could create the perfect ecosystem—the perfect place to build InJOYou, Inc., what would it look like? What would the landscape look and feel like? What would the climate be like? What would the community look like? What if you could custom design your ecosystem? Would your design look like the place where you are now, or would it look different? If your reality and your answers don't line-up, your ability to manufacture and distribute joy might very well be hindered by your current ecosystem more than your efforts!

So where do you start? What is the first step in custom designing an ecosystem that can grow, support, and sustain your joy? The first step is to make the choice to DARE 2B MORE…JOY-FILLED! The second step is to pour the foundational footers that will ensure your foundation can support your custom-designed ecosystem! The following chapters are devoted to teaching you how to do just that!

DARE 2B MORE… InJOYou.com

Chapter 6

The Seven Foundational Footers

They are like a man building a house, who dug down deep and laid the foundation on rock. When a flood came, the torrent struck that house but could not shake it, because it was well built. But the one who hears my words and does not put them into practice is like a man who built a house on the ground without a foundation. The moment the torrent struck that house, it collapsed, and its destruction was complete.
—Luke 6:48–49

It is not the beauty of the building you should look at: it's the construction of the foundation that will stand the test of time.
—David Allen Coe

My life has been a series of challenges, one right after another. I am not talking about the kind of challenges like passing a test, making the cheer team, learning to drive, getting a date for the prom, or figuring out what college I would attend. I wish those were my challenges! No! My journey has been one consumed by dark and malicious characters, widespread addiction, pathological liars, narcissism, child abuse, police, foster care, drugs, jail, sexual abuse, abandonment, teenage pregnancy, and more.

Truth is, I had planned to write my memoirs before I thought to write this book; I found the haunts of my past would lend themselves to pains of the present for far too many. Plus, my story is so dark it would be exhausting emotionally for me to write but also for others to read. After careful thought and consideration of my purpose for writing this book in the first place—to use my story to help others overcome—I concluded that the very best gift I could impart is that of wisdom. I dedicated this book to the "overcomer" because that is the best part of my story. I will share some of my trials as we turn the pages. My greatest desire is that the tools I've acquired will go with you. They have allowed me to build a grand staircase to a life that is now full of joy. I hope they will serve you in the same way.

I am not one to suggest another do something I have not already done. Three years ago, I took my master course, created my blueprint, and then built my InJOYou Inc.! It wasn't easy; anyone who says growth and change are easy is lying to you! Every challenge, struggle, and obstacle I endured was worth the price to achieve my dream—that of meeting the dawn of each new day with joy, peace, and love; all things I once believed would never be mine! Whatever you are going through, there is an excellent chance that I have experienced something similar. Please know I understand!

Although I have spent every year of my life since the age of seventeen working exponentially to be the kind of person others would label in a positive light, I continued to exist imprisoned by poor self-worth. I felt like a failure because my days and nights were plagued by misery, regardless of how hard I worked to be perfect.

There came a point when I had to acknowledge if drama, gloom and doom, and defeat, and dysfunction were my constant companions, then perhaps the real problem was me!

Accepting I was the true force behind this wildly insane, never-ending turbulent life, I took a long, hard look at myself. This was by far the most painful of my journeys. This journey demanded ownership for the role I had played in custom designing my current reality.

To others looking in, I was a great mom with wonderful kids, lived in a gorgeous home, traveled to great places, was self-employed, and full of confidence and sass. There were few, if any, goals I failed to bring to fruition. I taught my family and friends I was the person to call when the situation seemed impossible; I never failed in finding a way to get the job done. I was the poster child for self-confidence! Those closest to me knew the truth. I was a big fat fraud! My life was engulfed with pain, loneliness, sorrow, and constant uncertainty. I had lost the ability to dream of or to choose something better. The worst part was I had actively participated in the creation of the ecosystem literally killing me from the inside out.

The only hope I had left was to surrender and build a new ecosystem—one where I could begin to live again. Unfortunately, I was still me. I had the same belief systems that created everything I was desperate to flee.

Before I could even think about custom designing an ecosystem that could sustain my joy, I had to change what lived inside of me—the haunts, rage, guilt, doubts, bitterness, and insecurities. I had to find a way to uncage myself—to set my joy free. It was while doing the internal work to uncage myself that I discovered the seven foundational footers needed to support a dare 2b more…life. Whether you choose to custom design your ecosystem or not, these seven foundational footers, when applied, will change your life and exponentially increase your joy.

I want to share a secret with you. There is a key that unlocks the door to a joy-filled life. Each and every person in the world carries it with them at all times. Actually, it is a superpower! This is a superpower no one has earned; it was gifted to all human beings. It is a superpower we habitually reject and constantly abuse. I believe it so powerful it can be likened to having your own genie in a bottle. It is a superpower that can be used for good or sadly for evil but often can feel elusive or even obscure. So, what is this secret superpower we all have? Well, great surprises require a little suspense. Sorry…you will just have to keep reading a bit longer to find out!

The Rearview

You did not think I was just going to give up my secret that easily, did you?

I want you to dare 2b more…! I want you to know your best life. I want you to step fully into your intrinsic gifts and allow your strengths to become the tools that build stepping stools! I want this for you because a life without joy is simply unacceptable.

Deciding to embark on a road trip is only the first step of the journey. There are some decisions that have to be made before you go. When will you leave? What will you pack? Which direction will you head? How long will you be gone? What places will you see along the way? These are but a few of the decisions you need to make. However, the first decision is to select a destination. Only when you select a destination can you map the best route to get there. Of course, if you are more of a free spirit, you can just start driving, content to allow the road to determine where you go. But the fact remains: you still have to decide which road you're going to start driving down!

In the first pages of this book, I shared with you my love for airline travel. I illustrated what it looks like to live on purpose with purpose in the analogy of an airport traveler. I introduced you to two people who lived almost a century of life each, daring to be more! They chose to respond to life rather than waiting for something magically to come their way. Each intentionally chose with whom they would do life, where they wanted to do life, and how they responded to pain and opportunity when they came knocking! Like air travelers, Dorothea and Leroy lived their entire lives with purpose, on purpose! They knew the secret for a great life. They defined their lives rather than allowing life to define them.

They stayed in their lane by honoring their values and remained committed to joy rather than anguish. They could do this because they remained aware of who and what was in the lanes around them. As they're entering a season of narrowed years, both Leroy and Dorothea view their lives as blessed beyond measure! The smiles you see resonate from their souls—radiating light for the rest of us to bear witness, and if we are wise, follow their lead! They know joy, true unshakable joy. They live without keeping track of regrets! Can you imagine how it must feel to live with minimal regret, anxiety, and pain? *Freeing* is the word that shows up for me!

It is because of people like Leroy and Dorothea I developed a burning determination to figure out exactly how to custom design an ecosystem rooted in the purpose of joy. The countless hundreds of brilliant people I have sought as mentors throughout my years often shared a similar message of hope and inspiration. Great influencers all tend to say the same thing, *Find your purpose, find your passion, be motivated, work hard, keep moving forward, grow where you are planted, be determined, and, my personal favorite, learn to be content in the now.*

Their advice is awesome and pure truth!

What I really wanted to know was how? How was I supposed to build this beautiful life of abundance—that the collective "they" spoke—when I had made all the wrong choices for forty years? How was a forty-something supposed to create this utopian life at this stage of the game? Impossible! It was a novel idea but in practical application, little more than a pipe dream.

I sought the gurus hoping they could tell me point-blank where to start. What was step one? I never received an actionable answer that yielded the results for which I yearned. They all said the same thing, "Just take the first step." I hated that answer and still do for this reason—*What in the hell is the first step?*

I mean if I knew how to take the first step, then I would not be in the mess I am in…now, would I? I was frustrated because being the best person I could be and experiencing joy was at the top of my priority list. I was committed to doing whatever it took, but at the end of the day, all I got back was more of the same! Most of us just want a straightforward "how-to" manual—a map with a clearly marked route for how to get from where I am to where I want to go!

Since I could not find one, I designed one. I set out to create a road map that literally spelled out how to create your best life from the ground up step-by-step.

After I created the map, I discovered there was a flaw in my perspective. I took for granted I had invested years upon years of work into fixing me—a fact that made my map almost impossible for another to follow. I had been through years and years of deep self-analysis, had studied endless theories, read countless books, and had attended a nauseating number of courses and seminars and counselors. My design was no good because it could not serve you as it had me.

I heard a pastor on TV mention the word *pillars*! He spoke about the pillars of being a Christian.

Although I did not fully agree with his assessment, I did agree there had to be something like pillars each of us could construct or adopt to support the foundation of a dare 2b more…life.

In my work as an empowerment coach, I partner with clients to move them from where they are to where they want to be. Coaches work forward. On the other side of the coin, a counselor partners with their clients to uncover how they arrived at where they currently are. Counselors work backward. In my coach training, we are cautioned against walking our clients backward as a counselor would. In the interest of transparency and integrity, it is ethically inappropriate.

However, given my background, this seemed like an impossible task for me to fully adhere to if my mission was to help my clients create sustainable joy. Not everyone has experienced the massive train wreck I have, but we all have been shaped by our past experiences. That shaping is never perfectly round nor free of divots. It is for that reason people who have had an awesome life, as well as people who have had a bumpy road, sometimes…get stuck! (In case you are wondering what stuck looks like…it is living the same day, every day, without passion, excitement, purpose, fulfillment, or joy.)

My belief is that to become a truly healthy person, you must occasionally check the rear view! You must take a look at where you've been to gain clarity that where you're going is really where you want to go.

A support footer for a dare 2b more…life is not meant to be a checklist or a one and done. Support foundational footers are meant to be adopted into your everyday way of living. They are meant to shift your perspective so you can truly dare yourself to be more!

Think of these foundational footers as points on a map. If we were chatting and you asked me for directions, I could tell you how to get somewhere, but chances are you would get lost. Whereas, if I showed you the way, then not only could you find your way back, but you could also explore other ways to arrive at the same destination. The first time you move through the foundational footers, you need to pass by them in order! Once you pour foundational footers that are solid, when life gets a little bumpy, you will easily be able to check for any possible stress cracks and quickly repair them. Each footer brings with it a reward—greater freedom from anxiety, pain, and regret! Combined, they unlock your ability to custom design an ecosystem that can sustain InJOYou, Inc.! As I mentioned earlier, nothing of great value comes without a cost. The cost in this case is you are going to have to do the work and get comfortable being a little uncomfortable.

Integrating my personal knowledge, experiences, training, biblical truths, and the teachings of countless experts, I developed the following list of foundational footers needed to support a dare 2b more…life. I will break down each one in the chapters that follow.

Footer 1—Faith
Footer 2—Forgiveness
Footer 3—Accountability
Footer 4—Dreams
Footer 5—Intentional Choices
Footer 6—Acceptance
Footer 7—Mentors

DARE 2B MORE… InJOYou.com

Chapter 7

Footer 1—Faith

*Now faith is the confidence in what we hope for
and assurance about what we do not see.*
—Hebrews 11:1

Faith is believing in something when common sense tells you not to. Without faith a man can do nothing; with it all things are possible.
—Sir William Osler

The first footer to support a dare 2b more…life is faith. Before I dive into why, I want to give clarity to my personal viewpoint. Faith is not to be confused with religion; they are not the same.

"*Religion is not what manifests faith; religion is a vehicle you intentionally choose to communicate your faith. Religion is purposed to be an organized system to support and nurture a specific set of beliefs*" (Pastor Matt Dawson of Journey Church).

By now, I'm certain you are pretty darn clear that I am a person guided by my faith and for why I trust God as my CEO. But what you do not know is this was not always my truth!

When I think of faith, I naturally think of God. But there have been seasons in my life when I was far from God, when I could not feel his presence, and when I could not hear his voice, and frankly, did not really care that I could not. I did not grow up in an ecosystem that cultivated a Christian worldview (unless you want to include that of hypocrisy).

There were a few people in my life who talked about God or claimed that they believed in God and would occasionally force me into a church. From what I could see, God did not really seem like the kind of dude I wanted to hang out with on a Friday night!

He was judgmental, bossy, unrealistic in demands, conditional, and certainly had not protected me from experiencing immense abandon and pain, at least not in a manner identifiable to me. God, in all of his infinite "power and grace," had not intervened even one time to stop a single moment of the horror I witnessed or experienced. So why would I hope in a God that allowed so many people to physically, mentally, and emotionally hurt me over and over and over again?

How could I possibly trust an all-knowing, all-seeing commander in chief that I could not see or at the very least feel? Pain…Now that I could trust! I had plenty of proof for just how real that was. I secretly felt people of faith were ridiculous, delusional, and weak. I did not reject God, but I did not acknowledge or accept him either. I just did not "get" the whole God thing!

When I witnessed a person praying to their mysterious God—asking for wealth, healing, wisdom, guidance, etc.—I would think to myself, "Wait a minute. I understand this faith thing. God is like the elusive genie in the lamp—when you want something, you pray, and then go get it yourself but then give God the credit for your work. For that reason, I did not really see the value in prayer or faith or God! I'd proved that I was perfectly capable of getting what I wanted and needed, all by myself. I did not see the value in sharing the credit.

I did not reject God's existence; after all, I was not responsible for creation, nor could anyone else in history claim to be. I just did not see the point in placing my trust (i.e., hope and faith) in some genie-like entity, who clearly was not working on my behalf. If he was, then he sure had a funny way of showing his love for me, given I played the lead character in a never-ending horror series.

When I was a child, my mother had a framed poster hanging on the wall in the hallway of our home. It was called "Footprints in the Sand." It caught my attention one afternoon. I had walked past it a million times and never paid it a bit of attention, but for whatever reason, this one day I stopped and read it. When I got to the last stanza, the words "It was then that I carried you" brought me to tears. I had no explanation for why those combined words would bring me to tears, nor did I invest a second thought contemplating why. Interestingly enough, that poem resurfaced countless numbers of times throughout my years. Each time I saw it, the last stanza stirred my emotions. I always wondered why, until that one day, when I wondered no more!

I wish I could proclaim that I had some profound "come to Jesus" moment that changed my heart and forced me to my knees where God revealed himself to me and I came to faith! That would be some made-up crap! It just did not happen like that. My faith came to be through a series of trials where God showed up incognito and fixed the mess. I did not proclaim God as the victor during the storms back then, but I think somewhere deep down I must have always known he was responsible because there was no other explanation for the bad stuff turning out okay.

I met Patty at a school open house for our children who were entering kindergarten. Our sons were instantly best friends, and through a series of unique events, Patty and I also became like two peas in a pod. Patty was ultraconservative—almost uptight in my eyes. She had a great marriage and wonderful kids. She was uber educated, a thinker, slow to react, insanely detail-oriented, and filled with faith and love for God. She was raised in a completely "normal" family and cared little about having crazy adventures as I did!

I was her polar opposite. Our friendship made absolutely no sense! By what can only be explained as an act of God, we became the best of friends, so much so that her family unofficially, but quite officially, adopted me into their clan. We even became business partners, co-founding Workforce Echoes—an employee engagement consulting company.

Together there was not a problem we could not solve, including that of how I viewed the world and felt about my worth in it. Patty stood beside me in every moment of darkness and joy for more than ten years. She never judged me or put conditions on our friendship. She was the first person I unequivocally trusted. Patty believed in my potential as no other person had. She allowed me the space to be ridiculous, to wander around my thoughts, and to dream huge, seemingly impossible dreams. She was also my pain in the butt, voice of reason—one which I really needed!

During one of our many "girl therapy" sessions, I was venting about the overwhelming hurt I felt because I did not have a family of my own. (I was referring to my parents, grandparents, aunts and uncles, and cousins.)

Patty listened patiently in silence, as I poured out my vulnerability and self-pity. When she finally responded, her words had a profound impact on the way I viewed my world and God.

She said: "Sweetie, you may not have the mom or dad or family you desire, but what if you stopped focusing on that and started focusing on this instead? Families are not just the people to whom you were born. Families are the friends, who love you as if you were family…and isn't it better to be loved by people who choose to love you than by those who feel obligated to do so?"

As I said, she was my voice of reason!

So, what is my point? When Patty said those words, I thought about that poem that kept showing up, "Footprints." Instantly, my mind flashed across my whole life. I came to realize that in my lowest and darkest hours, Jesus had carried me through; I just did not know it at the time.

Jesus had carried me through the people he placed in my life—those who took care of me when I was alone or who showed me kindness or hugged me when I was scared and spoke words of love and encouragement into a little girl who felt so unworthy of receiving love. Jesus sent people who unexplainably showed up just in time to disrupt any intentions I had to take my last breath. He was in every stranger who encouraged and validated I was good enough or took the time to help with my homework or spared a few extra minutes to help me believe I was capable of achieving anything I wanted.

Jesus showed himself to me in the people, who were not my own yet showed up to provide a measure of care—care that allowed me to see what was possible and to believe, if only for a moment, that I could actually experience something good if I refused to give up! Something in me believed them!

Faith was not something I authentically leaned into, depended on, or genuinely accepted throughout most of my years. When I look back now, I may not have called myself faithful, but I guess I always had faith. I trusted against all the odds that things would be okay—that I would be okay! Deep down, I believed everything would work out even though there was so much evidence to the contrary. I had no reason to put my trust in man. The people who were charged with the responsibility of cultivating an emotionally safe space for me, had never done so; in fact, one by one, they each had abandoned me—leaving me alone in a dark and cold world.

I had no reason to believe things would be okay! Somehow, I made it through the bad stuff without becoming the person my parent's ecosystem dictated I should become. There is only one explanation for my being alive today, for being a good, loving, and compassionate person whose only purpose is to positively impact the lives of others; God took care of me in the storms! Because he did, I learned how to overcome, how to rise up, and how to use the gifts and talents He'd equipped me with to serve others. Hope gave me the courage to survive every dark hour. Hope was the key ingredient in making me different from that of my circumstances. God did not spare me from pain, but he did give me what I needed to endure it—a light in the darkness that helped me to navigate the way through.

I have had many people say to me if God loves you so much—if God is real—then why did you need to be carried through the storms in the first place? Why did you have to have the storms? There was a time when I struggled with those same questions. My answer may surprise you, but this is my truth.

When our parents separated, my sister and I were three and five. Through an insane course of events, I was raised by our mother and my sister by our father. We were forced to grow up completely void of the other, as though each of us were an only child. Not only were we void of our sister, we were also void of our other parent and the families they were born into.

My mother was an alcoholic and a prescription drug addict; she was incapable of being a mom. I became the adult when I was about five. That never changed. I took care of her through every binge and every adulterous affair and ensuing marriage (all six). I endured thirty-two school changes by my sophomore year. She forced me to see and experience things that no child should ever have too. The choices my mom made stole not only my innocence but my entire childhood. While the other kids were playing pretend with their dolls, I had to become the mother, that betrayal and addiction, held hostage from the little girl I so desperately wanted and needed to be.

My sister grew up in the exact opposite world. She had two parents, a normal and stable life, and lots of extended family and abundant love. Her life was the perfect picture of what I had most longed for, prayed for! Despite her seemingly picturesque life, my sister chose to walk a path of adversity and turmoil. You see my sister and my mom were exactly alike in how they reacted and responded to emotional pain. My sister was not built to endure the hell our mother created. I was! Our mother was not built to parent an out of control child. Our dad was! She had not chosen me instead of my sister as I once thought, but rather, I now believe that God placed me with her to protect her and to prepare me for the purpose he intended—to help and equip others with a set of tools to change their trajectory from unfulfilled to joy-filled. God knew that I could withstand what my sister most likely would not have endured well.

You see, that was always my purpose. It is what I was created for and have been doing my entire life even though I did not recognize my gifts were meant to serve a purpose, not my own! Was this fair? No! Do I wish our lives had been different? Of course! Was I a victim? Yes! But remember these truths in scripture: (1) God never promised easy to anyone. (2) God promised to love us, never abandon us, and to carry us through the storms. (Remember I spoke of all the people who loved me through.) (3) Jesus suffered, was rejected, and abandoned by his own people. (I am surely not worthy of less pain than the Savior who took on the sin of the world.) (4) God works all things for his good. If not for my storms, you would not be reading this book. If this book helps you, only you, then my storms were worth it! (It would take another book to share with you all the good that has come from the countless storms I have walked through.)

I have a tremendous faith in God. The religion that best supports my personal faith is non-denominational Christianity. My religion shapes, supports, and confirms my faith; it is not the reason my faith exists. My faith exists because of what my heart and mind have witnessed, not because a religious organization convinced me to believe in God or to proclaim faith. I place my faith in God, on purpose! I choose God because I have experienced life with him and without. Through the lens of my paradigm, during those seasons when I abandoned my faith in God, the paths I walked inevitably lead to canyons of pain and regret.

If God is not in whom you place your faith, then please do not allow our different choices to detour you from pouring this footer. Faith, as I said, is not about religious indoctrination. Faith is the foundation of hope. Hope is the vehicle that gives life meaning and keeps one moving forward when everything inside of them is screaming, quit. Without hope, sustainable joy is just not possible! Without hope, there is no reason to dream. Without hope, then what is left? We hope for love! We hope for success! We hope for good health and goodwill! We hope for the well-being of our family and our children! We hope for courage and forgiveness!

Like the word love, the word hope has morphed into a meaningless pleasantry, tossed about void of sincerity. When spoken with sincerity, you assert confidence and assurance that something you cannot see, control, or dictate will intercede on another's behalf to bring about a favorable outcome. That, my beautiful friend, is called faith!

Think of how many times a day you tell someone, I *hope* you have a great day, I *hope* everything works out, or I *hope* your health can be restored. Let me ask you something? In whom or what are you placing your hope in? Are you merely issuing a sentiment that is empty, or do you really believe that what you spoke hope for is possible? If your answer is the latter, then again, I ask you, in whom or what do you believe for the fulfillment of your hope? Hope and faith are one in the same. In whom or what we place our hope or faith is what may differ! I place my hope in God because only God—the creator of all things—is big enough to overcome the struggles I have faced. Only Jesus promises eternal joy—the joy that I most want to realize. Only God has stood the test of time! God is the only one who provides a literal road map for how to create, build, and live lives that can be sustained by joy throughout our time on earth (the Bible).

So…Here is the thing. Let's assume I am wrong! What have I lost by believing in God? What have I lost by trusting God and loving Jesus? What have I lost by adopting the values God commands in scripture—love, kindness, faithfulness, forgiveness, courage, understanding, compassion, care, peace, forbearance, goodness, hope, service to one another, humility, and self-control? (Self-control is what stops addiction, adultery, stealing, corruption, and the like.) Are any of these values bad for me, my children, my family and friends, or humanity? Are any of these things bad for you, your marriage, or your children or your neighbors? The better question would be what can you gain by having faith in God? The short answer is peace, joy, comfort, guidance, forgiveness, and truth and light!

Reread the list above and ask yourself this: What would your life look life if you had faith? What if you honored the values that God promises will lead to you living and leaving a legacy of joy? Would those you love, care for, work with, or walk through life positively benefit if you were to adopt God's values as your own?

Hope is trust! Faith is trust! If not hope, then what remains for people to trust in? If not faith in a higher power, then all that remains for you to place your hope in is man.

All people share the same limitation—we can't, without exerting force, control another person's behaviors or choices, nor can we speak life into being or stop death from coming. Hope is the opposite of control. Hope requires surrender. Hope is what we feel when we have no control over the outcome of a specific situation; yet, believe everything is going to be okay anyway!

I believe faith to be the one footer you cannot support a dare 2b more…life without because without faith, when life takes a swing at your joy, as it will over and over again, it will be your hope—your belief and assurance in that which you cannot see—that will get you out of bed and keep you moving forward with a spirit of joy.

Without a footer of faith, your dreams will struggle to survive the seemingly unsurmountable challenges that will assuredly arise as you dare to bring them to fruition! It is that simple! Sometimes, the only course of action you can take is to surrender in hope! Hope is faith!

It is ironic a person can go through their entire life rejecting God's existence, yet when they come face-to-face with an insurmountable pain or death, God is the only one who remains for them to place their hope in. Miracles really are possible! I'm living proof of that fact! Thankfully, the God I serve is in the business of making the impossible possible. Most who reject God do so because their miracle was, seemingly, withheld.

I recently learned a lesson I'd like to share with you. A friend of mine, who has faith beyond measure, asked God to give her family a miracle by saving her beloved aunt's life, a woman also deeply and passionately in love with the Lord. They prayed hourly, daily, and faithfully but in the end, God brought her aunt home. Devastated and heartbroken, those that were left behind found themselves angry with God.

I have felt the sting of death more times than I can count. I did not understand those losses any more than I did my friends. Some were tragic, some sudden, some expected, some heinous; none came with understanding nor without unbridled sorrow. The lesson I learned in trying to find words to comfort my brokenhearted friend was this: Maybe the miracle your aunt was praying for was greater than the miracle you most desired. Maybe God was not denying your miracle but granting hers. Also real but far less easy to digest, God has the best seat in the house; he can see the full picture. We only have a tiny, microscopic view. None of us can know what worse fate death may have spared our loved ones from experiencing. Jesus knows our tears; he lived first as man, feeling everything we feel, including that of pain, loss, and sorrow. Within the confines of my limited understanding, I believe Jesus brings people into our pain to remind us that we are not alone, have not been forgotten, nor forsaken.

It is not religion God demands of you. It is not perfection God requires of you. It is faith…that he asks of you! It is not God keeping you from joy; it is your need to be in control and your inability to surrender in faith that hinders your sustainable joy! Without faith, you will chase happiness—a pursuit that will always steal your joy and rarely bears the fruit you think it will.

Many would look at my life and draw the conclusion that I have lost far more than I have gained. They would be wrong. I have experienced hurt that could extend beyond the depths of the ocean. I have seen the face of evil up close and personal many, many times. I have every reason to be bitter, angry, untrusting, and leery of God's existence. I did not grow up in a church, nor was I raised by godly people, but the one thing I am certain of is this: I am not the person my circumstances dictated I should have become. I give credit to God alone for this truth. My village created the mass majority of my storms. I could have easily fallen prey and nearly did several times, but thankfully, God continually disrupted those plans. My paradigm is why my faith is unwavering.

On a scale of 1–10 (1, being not at all; and 10, being 100 percent), where would you rate your faith? To whom do you place your hope and trust? How has that been working out for you? What if you gave your trust and hope to God? What would that look and feel like for you? How could your life change if you allowed faith in a higher power to guide your values and choices?

DARE 2B MORE… BE FAITHFUL.

DARE 2B MORE… InJOYou.com

Chapter 8

Footer 2—Forgiveness

Do not judge, and you will not be judged. Do not condemn, and you will not be condemned. Forgive, and you will be forgiven. Give, and it will be given to you. A good measure, pressed down, shaken together and running over, will be poured into your lap. For with the measure you use, it will be measured to you.
—Luke 6:37–38 (NIV)

He that cannot forgive others breaks the bridge over which he must pass himself; for every man has need to be forgiven.
—Thomas Fuller

The Earth Quaked

I just got off the phone with my mother and grandfather, each on a different extension, both screaming wildly about how miserable the other is. Refereeing their battles was a weekly occurrence. I invested countless, exhaustive hours, days, weeks, months, and years dedicated to mediating their endless, hyperdysfunctional arguments. The frustration for me was the argument never changed. It was always a rehashing of the past—one I was trying desperately to forget. I tended to side with my grandfather; after all, he was the one person who had never lied to me, never hurt me, or betrayed me. I always believed he intended to steer my course in the right direction.

On this specific day, my grandfather called back immediately after we had just hung up. I cannot recall the context of the conversation, but that follow-up call changed every truth I had ever held. During our talk, I caught him in a lie. The context of the lie is irrelevant. What is important was the effect it had on me.

Later that week, I was talking with my best friend about the situation. Like a wrecking ball hurled into a glass monument, my heart shattered into a million pieces. I knew the vicious lie, told so many years ago, was anything but a lie. My worst fears came to fruition in the next call I received.

Travis from Eagle Valley Youth Ranch, where my eldest daughter had been receiving intensive, inpatient therapy for the past six months, called with the news I could never have dreamed in my worst nightmares, I would receive. "Hello! This is Travis. I'm sorry to have to make this call, but I need to inform you that we are opening an investigation with our local authorities into the sexual abuse of your daughter." I took a deep breath before very calmly uttering, "Who did it?" Travis replied, "I'm sorry. That is confidential." The next words out of my mouth were words I could not believe were my own. "It was my grandfather, wasn't it?" The line fell silent for a few moments before I heard, "Yes! It was! I'm sorry!"

There are no words that can communicate the impact of what I had to process in a split second. Anger, rage, devastation, confusion, guilt…you name it, the gang was all there, pounding in my head. I swear I felt the earth quake beneath my feet, knocking me to my knees. I had to call my mother.

She would be equally devastated to learn that her father—the appointed hero of our little family—was a demonic child molester who'd preyed on those who called him daddy, granddaddy, and great-granddaddy. My mother had been living in my grandparents' home since the passing of my grandmother. I wondered how she could not have known. How could she not have seen it?

In recent years, she had warned me of signs that indicated she thought he may have an unhealthy obsession with my daughter—warnings I had vehemently rejected because my mother spent most of her days slumped over and strung out on pain pills. There was also the fact that she loved to create dramatic problems where none previously existed.

(Side note for added perspective of the situation: My mother did get sober for a short time. During that time, she became a dual diagnosis addictions counselor, but her sobriety ended soon after she moved in with her father. My stepfather was also an addictions counselor employed at, of all places, a psychiatric institute. Because my daughter was such a difficult child, and I did not have a support system, I would send her to spend a few weeks of the summer with my grandfather, mom, and stepfather. I sent her there because I believed she would be safer and happier in the care of my grandfather than in the care of random strangers. I knew he would enroll her in all sorts of fun activities that I could never do on my own.)

The fact was just moments before that call, not one of us would have dreamed of uttering as truth that *my grandfather—my hero—* was a sexual deviant who preyed on the children of our family. How could this be happening?

"Hello, Laura, what's going on?"

"Mom, I have to tell you something. I just got a call from my daughter's counselor. Granddaddy has been sexually molesting her since she was six years old. (She was now seventeen.) He physically violated her until she was eleven and has been emotionally abusing her since then."

As if those words I had just spoken were not devastating enough, the three words my mother said next, yet again, dropped me to my knees in physical agony. In an almost celebratory tone, my mother proclaimed, "I knew it!"

My anger turning to full outrage, I screamed, "WHAT? What do you mean you knew it? You knew it, and you did nothing to stop it? You didn't tell me?" I was so angry that I cannot recall with any accuracy her next words or even my own.

What I have not yet shared is what the lie was—the one I mentioned earlier. Eighteen years prior to this, my little cousin, who was more like a little sister, told her mom (my aunt and my mother's sister) that our grandfather had molested her.

At that time, it also came out my grandfather had molested my aunt when she was a child. My aunt told my great-grandmother what he had done to her. My great-grandmother responded, "Never breathe a word of this to your mother because it will kill her." My aunt never told. When my cousin brought her horror to light, no one in our family, myself included, believed her. My cousin and her parents were immediately exiled for making such horrific accusations against the patriarch of our family. Charges were never pressed, and it was never spoken of again. The lie was never a lie.

My family shattered in one phone call; our lives laid in ruin. My heart and soul were ravaged by anger so intense I lack an adequate vocabulary to convey its measure. I wanted revenge; I wanted to unleash my wrath upon the world—upon those members of my tribe, accountable for protecting the innocence of our families most vulnerable. Never had I wanted anything more than to inflict immense physical pain upon him as justice for his crimes. We had all been violated in the worst possible way. But the truth was my family was shattered the day my aunt's voice was silenced. If that evil had not occurred, four generations would not have endured the horror we did. I had to do something to stop this madness and make him pay for all he had taken from each of us.

I located my long-lost cousin, begged for her forgiveness and then pleaded for her help in pursuing the justice that would hold our grandfather accountable for his crimes. Together, we joined the prosecutor's pursuit in righting these wrongs. My mother, on the other hand, chose a side—his side. Our relationship all but ended that day! The minute I sought his conviction, I lost my grandfather, mother, stepfather, and stepsister. They were the only family I had known since I was thirteen years old. Although I gained my cousins and aunt, we were strangers among family; the trial took a toll on the rebuilding of our familial connection.

After a two-year, exhaustive trial, my grandfather was found guilty of sexual assault at eighty-four years of age.

Immediately following the conviction, I waited for my grandfather in the parking lot of the courthouse. He was accompanied by a USN Retired Vice Admiral who had come to support him. I confronted him, screaming at the top of my lungs hoping I could restrain myself from inflicting the physical pain that bore the depth of the scars he had callously carved into the hearts of four generations of women in my family. Hatred seeped through every pore of my body. I wanted revenge. I wanted him to feel the magnitude of fear and hurt that my daughter carried, but more than that, I wanted answers. I wanted to know why and how someone I loved and trusted so completely could steal my child's innocence and destroy our family. But the louder I screamed, the louder he and the vice admiral screamed back. I quickly realized, short of doing something that would land me in prison, there was nothing he or I could say that would even begin to ease the agonies ravaging my heart and soul. I stood there totally alone, shattered, and with tears clouding my vision, as my once hero turned archenemy drove away a free man, battling to accept that there was nothing left that I could do but to walk away and begin again.

The next ten years of my daughter's life (and consequently mine) were fraught with mass dysfunction—the kind only promiscuity, heroin, and crime yield. She gave birth to a son. As a result of her addiction, he and she were dragged through unspeakable circumstances. Just beyond his second birthday, I convinced my daughter to place her beautiful son up for adoption with a wonderful family that was willing and able to give him the life he so deserved. I'll never forget the magnitude of heartache I felt watching that car back out of my driveway, taking with it my first grandchild—the one I watched take his first breath. It felt as though I had just buried my own child. My daughter spiraled even further out of control. Losing my precious grandson while at the same time knowing my daughter was teeter-tottering on the edge of certain death only deepened the hatred within me. My mother and grandfather had ransomed my father, sister, my family, my childhood, me, my daughter, and now my innocent grandson in exchange for nothing of value, nothing more than their own sick and twisted desires. Those of my own blood were responsible for every tear that fell from my eyes. I blamed them for every pain thrust upon us. Even now, as I write these words, I can't fight back the flood of tears streaming down my face.

A little over a year after my precious grandson left my home for the last time, I watched as my daughter signed the final adoption paperwork. Seven months later, she gave birth to her second son, but on the heels of his third birthday, she lost custody of him to her ex-husband—also an addict—as a result of her continued drug addiction and propensity for crime. She overdosed countless times and spent two years in and out of jail—the longest stretch being six months. Her scars were deep and wide and many. But by God's protection and unfailing grace, today, she has been off drugs and out of jail for better than two years. She's engaged to a wonderful guy, and once again is a mother to her son.

I believed once he was convicted—once justice had been served—I would be "good," and I would be able to fix everything as I always had been able to do. I had to believe I could make it all "good" again. That was a delusion.

The guilt and shame, anger and resentments, and the total devastation of my family had changed me into someone I did not want to be. When I looked into the mirror, the reflection was void; I was but an empty shell of a woman ravaged by anger and hate. I was angry at my family, God, and the world. In all truthfulness, the person I hated the most was me.

Each day, my daughter answered the call of addiction to flee the haunts of her past was a reminder that I had failed her, just as my mother had failed me. Because of my failure, her life, the lives of her children, and mine painted a picture of more hell than heaven—a hell that seemed to be without end. That was my burden to carry, and I can assure you the weight of it was crushing me, but I had two incredible and deserving younger children that needed the very best of me. I could not fail them, as I had failed their sister.

To others, on the outside, I looked strong, confident, capable, and basically happy. I was so good at pretending that everything was fine, that life was good, that even I believed the lies. My two little ones became my entire universe. I was hell-bent that they would never suffer as their sister or I had. I made a promise the day they were born that they would experience the best of everything. They were the only light in a very dark and lonely world. But even for them, the love I had to give felt insufficient. Something had to give.

My husband decided that a family trip was the medicine I needed to cure my broken heart. During the long journey back home, I stared out the window numb to all emotion. I happened to notice a billboard for Love's Country store! My mother's face flashed before my eyes; for years, she had carried a Love's mug with her everywhere she went. It was like her signature garment. I had not seen a Love's Country store since moving from the Midwest many, many years ago. I did not give it much more thought, but unfortunately, now my mom was on my mind. We had not spoken since my grandfather's arrest almost three years ago. A few miles later, I noticed a directional sign to Norfolk. My family lived in Norfolk. A few miles more there was a small sign for a town that shared my mother's last name. Still a few more miles passed, and there was a billboard that said something about forgiveness! Suddenly, I was intensely angry.

God was placing it on my heart to forgive that child-molesting evil monster, who had devastated my family for generations. Not only was this man responsible for ripping my daughter and grandson from my life but also my father, sister, grandparents, aunts, uncles, and cousins. I grew up fatherless and sisterless because of the cult he set out to build before I was even born. He was at the core of every single pain I held; he authored the evil that penetrated five generations.

I rationalized the coincidence of these "signs." Faith and hate went to war inside my mind. I remember thinking, *Hell…no!* There is no way I had the capacity to stand in front of that man, in my childhood home, the very same one where my cousin and daughter had been violated by my once hero and say the words, "I forgive you!" "No just *no*…Not going to happen God!"

That was just too much to ask of me. Maybe *he* could forgive that monster, but I sure as hell could not. This was the conversation I had with God over the next four hours. I wish I could tell you what changed my mind, but I really do not know. What I did know was that if I did not go and forgive him and my mother alike, I would never be free—free to laugh, love, trust, or be the wife, mother, and friend I was meant to be. I had to reclaim the power I had given them over my emotions, love, and goodness. It dawned on me that by remaining devastated, emotionally bankrupt and unavailable, and isolated from joy, I was rewarding their crimes by giving them the best parts of me. At the same time, I was punishing the people who had done no wrong by withholding the limitless love and joy I wanted to give them.

The next morning, I got in my car, drove four hours, and entered that house of pain. With tears flooding down my face, barely able to speak a single word, I looked into my grandfather's eyes and said the hardest words I have ever spoken, "I forgive you! I forgive you for sexually molesting my aunt, cousin, and daughter. I forgive you for enabling my mother's addiction and for watching as she devastated my childhood. I forgive you for separating me from my father and sister. I forgive you for convincing my mother to marry my uncle and have him adopt me. I forgive you for stealing my joy as a child, daughter, granddaughter, wife, mother, and grandmother. I forgive you for stealing my child's innocence and for authoring and ushering in evil for every member of our family. Lastly, I forgive you for failing as my hero."

I listened for a moment as he and my mother began to verbally attack me for what they called "vicious and outrageous lies." I considered the sheer audacity of my mom uttering even a single syllable in anger toward me, given the train wreck of a mother she had been my entire life. I wish I could say her betrayal was unexpected, but never was I her priority. I wanted to engage; I wanted to lash out with all the hatred and venom I could call up. I wanted to spit in his face and curse him to the heavens, but I knew I had to hear their side to truly grant them my forgiveness. I stood there, and I took their verbal abuse. It took every ounce of prayer, faith, and restraint I could muster to silence the voice of violence welling up inside of me. Instead, I once again uttered the words, "I forgive you."

When I released the words "I forgive you," a peace came over me. It was faint, but I could feel it. Forgiveness can only be given without condition, but to do that meant I had to surrender my anger to God. It was by my faith alone I emerged victorious in my mission.

I interrupted them both stating, "I came to forgive you, and I have done that. I will never allow either of you a space in our lives again. I will never forget your deeds, but I do forgive you, and it is my prayer God will forgive you too." I said, "Goodbye!" and drove four hours back home to hug my children! From that day forward, the hurt, anger, and bitterness no longer had any power to restrict my love from those who were innocent.

I have shared this story with you in such detail because I want you to know I understand what it is to be consumed with so much shame, guilt, and anger you feel as if you are suffocating—as if nothing will ever be right or good again. I understand how hard it is to trust again after someone betrays you. I understand how hard it is to forgive the smallest of offenses, let alone the worst of crimes. I get it—truly I do!

Please believe me when I share with you that if you do not find a way to forgive others and yourself, to ask for forgiveness from God and those you have wronged, you will forever live confined by the chains of emotional bondage. Those haunts will separate you from experiencing the fullness of peace and joy you most want. Don't cheat yourself from experiencing your best and most joy-filled life because you refuse to let go of your past demons. It doesn't matter if you are the victim or the victimizer; Jesus died on the cross for payment of our sin—mine, theirs, and yours.

The secret to forgiveness is to accept that it is a gift, and sometimes you will have to give it away again and again. You do have a choice in who and what you give your power to. Don't think for a second that you don't.

If you want your tomorrow to feel different than your yesterday, then you have to choose to change how you feel today! The sun can and will shine on you again; your willingness to forgive and be forgiven is what will determine when.

Let the "stuff" of yesterday go before it steals anymore of your joy, happiness, and peace. Holding on is not worth the ultimate cost to your soul!

If you are a victim of sexual abuse, physical abuse, mental abuse, emotional abuse, it is not your fault. You do not deserve it. You are valuable! Your life and your gifts are worthy and deserving of your honesty. Do not listen to the lies of those who say, "You cannot tell because others will not believe you." If someone is hurting you, tell everyone; scream it from the rooftops until someone listens. There is no shame in telling someone what has been done to you. If you do not tell, not only will your life be lived in silent suffering, but the lives of your children and their children very well may be, too. Child predators are the most horrific kind of thieves because what they steal is a child's soul. Once a child's soul has been stolen, getting it back can be next to impossible. There is help! There are people who will listen and believe you and love you and support you. You are not alone! If you cannot find someone to help you, reach out to me, I will! (://www.childhelp.org)

You may not share my faith or my beliefs, but the fact remains your anger for those that have wronged you or your guilt for having wronged others is separating you from living a life of joy. If you hold on to guilt, anger, and hurt, you are cheating yourself of the freedom to give and receive love. Where there is no love, there can be no joy! This is the reason why the second footer in a dare 2b more… life is forgiveness. You must release yourself from the pains that are holding your joy hostage before you can be emotionally free to build InJOYou, Inc.!

We are emotional beings, each with our own unique communication style and sinful nature. This allows a tremendous amount of space for others to make us feel wronged. Feeling wronged causes an explosion in our hearts, forcing our brains to enter what I call firefighter mode. Our minds rush to save our heart from the flames. When someone, especially one you love, wrongs you regardless of how insignificantly, you enter a state of fight or flight. You may become angry and retaliate in word or deed, leaving you feeling guilty or regretful. You may retreat, withhold your time, voice, or love, which leaves you alone with your pain. You may be a person who does both. What is certain is your feelings are hurt, your trust is injured, and often your worth comes into question.

Wrongs can be likened to bricks. With each wrong you endure, another brick is added to the proverbial wall around your heart—a wall purposed to protect your emotions. We build emotional walls in response to our hurt feelings, hoping they will protect us from being hurt yet again. The more we are hurt, the faster we build. There are two problems with building emotional walls—walls intended to hold others at bay. One, they will not prevent you from wanting to be the person you intrinsically are or from wanting to show up for others as you most desire. Two, emotional walls imprison your love, joy, gifts, and talents right next door to your pain. The longer your love and joy remain imprisoned, the harder it becomes to give and receive the very love and light you are longing to know. Forgiveness is what conquers hurt; refute it, and your hurt is all that will remain.

Before we can move on to the next footer, we need to talk about what forgiveness is and what it is not! This is simply too important of a footer to get wrong! That is why I am diving deeper, belaboring the point, and pleading with you to dare 2b more…forgiving—of yourself and others!

What Forgiveness Is

Forgiveness is an intentional choice to voluntarily give another person the same compassion and grace you want for yourself. Easier said than done. I know! Here's the deal. You don't need easy; you only need possible!

Nancy Colier, a psychotherapist, interfaith minister, author, public speaker, mindfulness teacher, and relationship coach, wrote in her article "What Is Forgiveness Really?"

> *Forgiveness is in part a willingness to drop the narrative on a particular injustice and to stop telling ourselves over and over again the story of what happened, what this other person did, how we were injured, and all the rest of the upsetting things we remind ourselves in relation to this unforgivableness. It is a decision to let the past be what it was, to leave it as is, imperfect and not what we wish it had been. Forgiveness means we stop the shoulda, coulda, woulda beens, and relinquish the idea that we can create a different (better) past.*

The "why" to forgive has absolutely nothing to do with justice and absolutely everything to do with freedom—your mental, physical, emotional, and spiritual freedom. According to an article published by John Hopkins Medicine,

> *Studies have found the act of forgiveness can reap huge rewards for your health, lowering the risk of heart attack; improving cholesterol levels and sleep; and reducing pain, blood pressure, levels of anxiety, depression, and stress. Research points to an increase in the forgiveness-health connection as you age.*

> *There is an enormous physical burden to being hurt and disappointed," says Karen Swartz, M.D., director of the Mood Disorders Adult Consultation Clinic at The Johns Hopkins Hospital. Chronic anger puts you into a fight-or-flight mode, which results in numerous changes in heart rate, blood pressure, and immune response. Those changes then increase the risk of depression, heart disease, and diabetes, among other conditions. Forgiveness, however, calms stress levels, leading to improved health.*

It is a natural response to feel angry when anyone, especially those we love or care for, choose behaviors that lay pain at our feet. Anger activates your fight-or-flight response. This protective instinct alerts your mind that a defensive posture is immediately required. The state of anger is both protective and destructive. Why? By its very nature, anger ignites you to take immediate action—to respond right now. How you respond will either be constructive or destructive to your joy. At the moment of impact—the moment someone wrongs you or you wrong another—how you respond is a choice. If you choose to respond in kind, then you are, in essence, choosing to pour gasoline on the fire. If you choose the path of forgiveness, it's likened to dousing the flames with water.

Negative emotions separate you from joy. Hostility, disappointment, regret, shame, guilt, fear, anger, and hurt are the valleys that force you to climb another mountain. Regardless of how intentionally you design InJOYou, Inc., at some point, life will serve each of us a portion from this buffet. Life is hard! That is an inescapable and undeniable truth. But also true is that in every valley, in every storm, you have a choice in how you respond—in the person you choose to be.

When your anger leads you down the path of vengeance, you are not only separated from joy but also from the best version of yourself. It takes an exponential amount of focus and energy to maintain a state of anger. From where does that extra energy come? Well, it comes from every division at InJOYou, Inc.—your relationships, passions, career, health, finances, creativity, curiosity, and faith. Anger is the opposite of joy. To maintain anger, you have to stop manufacturing joy. Once you stop production, then InJOYou, Inc., will quickly run out of joy to distribute. Your entire business will be impacted, and your ecosystem will begin to grow weeds!

Forgiveness is like the oil that keeps the machines of InJOYou, Inc., running smoothly and at full capacity. Please understand forgiveness is a choice, but…it is also a gift. Have you ever given a gift to someone with the expectation they were going to give it back? Gifts are not given with the intention to take them back. Forgiveness is a gift! If your plan is to take back your gift, don't bother giving it in the first place.

It never fails when I teach on forgiveness, someone will say, "Forgiveness is earned. I didn't do anything wrong. They need to ask for forgiveness before I give it to them." This mindset creates the space to justify withholding one's forgiveness. These are the lies we tell ourselves so we can hold onto our venom a little while longer. Because we feel wronged, we also feel a measure of entitlement to vindication. What you need to remember is that your bitterness will not erase what has already been done. It will not change another person's choices, nor does harboring resentments impact the trajectory of those who have wronged you. What it will do is change your trajectory from joy-filled to unfulfilled. By holding onto your hurt, you're empowering it to determine your level of happiness and joy. To hold onto wrongs means that you have to keep replaying the tapes over and over again. To withhold forgiveness is to forfeit your joy into the hands of those who have hurt you.

The ones who struggle the most with this footer are those who immediately recognize they are most in need of forgiveness. The people who decide that confessing their sins will yield more pain and loss are the ones who struggle the most with pouring this vital joy-building footer. They cannot look past the messiness long enough to realize that while the truth does often offend, it is the key that unlocks their emotional freedom. I would encourage those who are afraid that confessing their truths might yield unbearable consequences to ask themselves these tough questions. What joys, opportunities, love, and peace are you missing out on because the chains of fear bind you? Which of your gifts, strengths, and talents do you deny because you are afraid? How many relationships or opportunities have you lost or rejected because of guilt, shame, and fear? Do you turn away from your reflection because to look into it is a reminder that you are no longer who you want to be? What would you do if you weren't afraid of feeling retribution, rejected, foolish, or alone? What if… every hope and dream you desire are denied because you exhaust your energy running, hiding, concealing, and deflecting the haunts of your story? How would it feel to let go of baggage holding you back? How would it feel to be set free from the chains that you have built link by link?

It is this simple. Forgiveness is a choice. It is a gift—one that may need to be given away many times over; sometimes those to whom we gift it, give it back! Forgiveness is a four-step process; it is not simply saying the words "I forgive you." Authentic, sustainable forgiveness starts with forgiving those who have wronged you and then asking for forgiveness from those you have wronged. Next you need to seek God and ask his forgiveness over the entire situation. Lastly, you have to forgive yourself. That is often the hardest of the four steps. Forgiveness is like a ladder that drops from the top of the mountain down into the valley. It will lead you out, but not until you begin the climb to reach it.

There is nothing you have done or has been done to you that God's grace and mercy cannot overcome! Opening the door that held captive the many haunts throughout my story was both overwhelming and terrifying. Forgiving those whose crimes had cost me dearly felt backward and mostly impossible. Coming to terms with the fact that the internal cages I built to punish the monsters that haunted me were the very same cages holding the best of me hostage—holding my joy hostage—gave me great clarity regarding the power of forgiveness. I had willingly cast myself in the leading role of a prisoner in my story. Once I fully understood this, I began to rewrite the script, starting with "And all at once…she tore down the walls exchanging her pain for peace and joy." But there was a plot twist on the horizon… My leading lady, me, had to confront and take ownership that she was not without blemish or blame for the pains of the past. I could not have done any of that without God's strength guiding me.

I had to humble myself and ask many, including my own children, to forgive me of my wrongs. I had to ask my eldest daughter to forgive me for failing to protect her, for failing to see what was happening, and for failing to be the mother she deserved and needed me to be. I had to get honest with myself regarding my accountability for the circumstances that defined my story. Trust me when I say, taking one's own inventory is far more agonizing than exposing another's.

I had to then sit before God and admit that I needed to be forgiven for the sins of my thoughts, actions, and deeds that went unnoticed by anyone other than me. Cleaning out the trunk is a nasty, dirty, tough job. But when it is finished, *wow*…that trunk really shines brightly! But more than that, the peace, freedom, and joy that flows from it, is like nothing I can articulate.

Forgiveness is the second foundational footer in a dare 2b more…life because your emotional baggage is, and will continue to hold your joy hostage. It is making you sick, mentally, emotionally, and physically! InJOYou, Inc., cannot manufacture and distribute a product of joy until you make the choice to oil the machines.

We cannot talk about what forgiveness is without taking a few minutes to address what it is not.

What Forgiveness is *Not*

I would be remiss to encourage forgiving someone of their wrongs or you of yours without adding clarity to what forgiveness absolutely *is not*. I believe the reason most of us struggle with forgiveness is we somehow feel some wrongs are simply too infinite to let go of or that some wrongs are unworthy of our forgiveness. How can you forgive someone who took everything and betrayed you so deeply that your heart aches every day? How can you forgive a person whose acts are pure evil and completely unjustified? You may be thinking, sure it is easy to forgive someone for being a jerk, lying, or even cheating but to forgive someone for murder, rape, abuse, addiction, abandonment, or molesting your child—these are crimes that do not deserve to be forgiven. You are not wrong, but you are not right either!

"For in the same way you judge others, you will be judged, and with the measure you use, it will be measured to you" (Matthew 7:2 NIV). This is why it is so important to make the distinction between what forgiveness is and is not. Remember forgiveness is a choice and a gift that is for your freedom, not that of another. Here is what forgiveness is not:

- Forgiveness is *not* a release for the consequences of your actions. It is not a hall pass for injustice.
- Forgiveness does not mean granting permission to or for anyone to hurt you repeatedly, mentally, physically, emotionally, or spiritually, nor does it mean granting permission to yourself to inflict harm upon any other person.
- Forgiveness does not mean that a person who has hurt you can actively remain in your life as they once did. Sometimes, you will need to forgive and let go of a person who is toxic to your joy even if you deeply love them. That is okay!

Some people are only meant to come into your life for a reason and a season! As the old saying goes, "Fool me once, shame on you. Fool me twice, shame on me!"

- Forgiveness is not an exchange of permission to remain in a situation where you are being violated, or abused, or treated in ways that cause emotional or physical pain for you, your children, or your loved ones. Toxic people are like weeds or cancers within InJOYou, Inc. If you do not remove them, then they will take over your ecosystem and destroy your joy. But if you do not forgive them, then your bitterness, resentments, and anger will be the weeds that destroy InJOYou, Inc.

- Forgiveness does not eliminate personal accountability or responsibility for the role you, personally, have played in the creation of the situation or circumstance that warrants forgiveness. The buck stops with you. You are not a victim even if you have been victimized because you are in control of how you choose to respond to your circumstance. An employee says, "I can't because…" A COO says, "I can because…"

- Forgiveness does not mean you will or should ever forget. I will never forget what my grandfather did, what he took, or how he betrayed us all. He was never allowed a place in my world again. Because I never forgot, I became more aware of the evils that lurk around every corner. I became more educated about how to protect my children and how to communicate with them about sexual predators. I engaged in new and better conversations with my children, creating a safe space for them to come to me, should anyone attempt to harm them, in any way. I talked with other parents about what I went through so they could watch for signs of sexual abuse with their own children. I learned how to have more grace with my daughter and how to better support her through her struggles.

I also taught my daughter how to forgive her demons because although he had been convicted and could no longer hurt her, the wounds he inflicted remained. It was not until she could forgive him, forgive herself, forgive me, and any other she felt had failed in protecting her that she was finally set free to love herself, her son, and another!

- Forgiveness is not for the benefit of the person(s) who wronged you; it is for the benefit of the person you most want to be! Forgiveness is not only a gift that you give to another, it is a key that you gift to yourself to set your joy free!

There is another aspect of forgiveness that might be hard for you to accept, dependent upon your paradigm. To truly forgive someone, you must also allow a space for the other person to be heard. Compassion cannot exist where there is no understanding. Again, understanding is not condoning negative, toxic, or evil behavior. Understanding is part of the process of forgiving. I cannot condone what was done to my child. But I needed to understand how my grandfather could be both a hero and villain. To truly free myself from the hatred I felt for him, I needed to understand the why.

My grandfather was also a victim of unimaginable abuse. He grew up in an environment where he was unmercifully beaten by his stepfather, day in and day out, receiving no protection from those who were commissioned to do so. He endured extreme poverty and abuse throughout his entire childhood. He learned that "love" meant hurt, secrecy, lies, deceptions, illusions, domination, and control. My grandfather, like so many who are abused, was a victim before he became a victimizer.

My grandfather was also a Lieutenant Commander in the US Navy. He flew jets off aircraft carriers and witnessed wars, destruction, and death! When he retired from the only life he had known, chronic depression took over his mind. The preferred treatment of that generation was electroshock therapy; for three years, the doctors fried his brain rendering him almost vegetative. Ironically, it was after this that he pursued and obtained a bachelor's degree in, of all things, psychology.

His paradigm in no way, shape, form, or fashion can justify his crimes nor grant him freedom from the accountability and consequences of his choices. His childhood cannot excuse the horror he inflicted on our family. However, knowing what he lived through helped me to have just enough compassion to forgive him. It allowed me a deeper understanding for what led to his becoming the horrific villain I never imagined he could be. Understanding is not excusing, but it is a pathway that can afford you just enough compassion to grant forgiveness when it seems impossible to do so!

Who do you need to forgive? What grievous action was taken against you that you need to forgive? How would it look or feel if you did? From whom would you like to receive forgiveness and for what? How would it look or feel if they gave it you? What if you asked God to forgive you, to forgive those who have wronged you? What if emotional freedom is only one act of forgiveness away?

DARE 2B MORE… BE FORGIVING.

DARE 2B MORE… InJOYou.com

Chapter 9

Footer 3—Accountablility

It is written:
"As surely as I live," says the Lord, "every knee will bow
before me; every tongue will acknowledge God."[a]
So then, each of us will give an account of ourselves to God.
—Romans 14:11–12

The moment you take responsibility for everything in your life
is the moment you can change anything in your life.
—Hal Elrod

"I didn't have a choice!" How many times have you heard that? How many times have you uttered those words as a justification for your choices? "I did not have a choice" is a leading excuse for living without accountability. It separates you from a life of joy and is a complete cop-out! "I didn't have a choice" translates to "I value pain more than joy."

By age fifteen, I had witnessed more carnage than most eighty-year-old adults. I had seen the face of evil up close and personal so many times that I felt like Satan himself had identified me as one in need of his personal attention! At the tender age of fifteen, I was a force to be reckoned with. I did what I pleased, and if you got in my way, you got moved! I was angry and hell-bent on rebellion. My theme song was Janet Jackson's "Control"!

Like her, "I was going to do it my way."

Miraculously, as broken and damaged as I was, I still believed there was something in me that was different from those with whom I associated—maybe even something good or special. I genuinely and deeply cared for the well-being of others. There was little I would not do to help a stranger and always tried to make things better for those around me. I was a servant leader; I just did not know it!

During one of my mom's many blackouts, she asked a man named Jeb to come to our home. Reluctantly, when he knocked on our garage door, I allowed him in despite knowing the real reason my mother had extended this invitation. As anticipated, my mother cast her seductive net and lured this gullible man into the same bedroom she shared with my adoptive father and seduced him. I remember sitting in the other room, seething with anger as I covered my ears, desperate not to hear the moans of sexual pleasure emoting from my parent's bedroom. Even though I had only just met him, I felt hatred for him, and the repulsion I felt for my mother only deepened.

It came as little surprise that not long after their meeting, my mother filed for what would be her fifth divorce and soon married Jeb, who had left his wife of twenty-seven years and his four children to marry my mother! Our latest "happy little family" moved to a new town and into a one-bedroom apartment. I was forced to transition from a 3,600-square-foot home with a beautiful pool and a basement I could roller-skate in, to sleeping on a mattress in the tiny living room of our four-room apartment. Our adventure in Dodge City would prove to be just one more chapter in a seemingly never-ending saga of pain.

One afternoon, I arrived home from work to find my belongings on the street in front of our house. As tears of rage welled up in my eyes, I could only draw one conclusion; my mother had caught me! I had disobeyed her direct orders, and obviously, she knew it.

I was fourteen; I had just gotten my learner's permit and graduated from the eighth grade. Joe, my adoptive father, bought "me" a brand-new 1986 Mazda RX-7 as my graduation present! (Truth was he only did it to tick off my mom; he brilliantly succeeded.) When she learned of the car, I was told in no uncertain terms I was not to drive it, period. I generally did not make a habit of taking her on, but by this point, I did not give two cents about what she wanted. I was going to drive my new sports car. (What fourteen-year-old wouldn't when presented with an option to do so?) After all, Joe was my dad by her own design so that meant when I was with him, he was in charge. She said, "No," He said, "Yes!" I followed the yes! My punishment for this heinous crime was…banishment! I gathered my things and I bunked up with my neighboring friend until my father finally showed up to take me back to my hometown. By then, I had had enough—enough pain, enough heartache, enough of it all. I just wanted the noise to stop.

I had changed schools thirty-two times by the start of my sophomore year. I was strong-willed and rebellious as all get out! I figured out how to work systems and manipulate people to get what I wanted. Drinking, drugs, and boys filled the void I existed in. Sometime after Christmas break, I cut school to go party with another girl and our boyfriends. After several hours of making some rather poor choices, we eventually returned to school.

Almost immediately upon my return, I was halted by Mr. Thomas, the assistant principal. He called me into his office to chat about my day. He was kind and tried to save me from myself, but my soul was empty. I just did not care about anything anymore. My family had pounded it into my head that I was worthless. I agreed with them. I informed Mr. Thomas I was dropping out of school until the following fall.

I will never forget his words: "Please don't do this! If you do, you will never return, and your life will be forever ruined." Dear God, how I wish I would have known the truth he spoke that day. For if I could go back and speak to my younger self, I would have saved her from that horrible moment of impact.

That moment was pivotal because this time, the consequences were mine to bear alone!

I was only fifteen—too young to quit school—so I went to an alternative school, otherwise known as "The school for the colossally stupid!" I had rung a bell that could not be unrung.

One night after class, I was having a drink of Johnny Walker with my father. He was going on and on about his incessant desire for my mom—the same woman who divorced him three times to marry other men. Bored of his whining and a bit tipsy, I passed out on the couch. I awoke to my father kissing me, running his hands across my stomach and down my pants. My tipsiness turned to full-on rage. I shoved him off me, grabbed the JW bottle, and hurled it toward him. Unfortunately, I missed; it shattered into a million pieces upon contact with the bookcases. I grabbed my shoes and stormed out. I had no intention of ever returning. Everyone who was accountable to love and protect me had hurt and abandoned me. I was fifteen and alone.

Feeling I had no value, I attempted to take my life by overdosing on pills. That choice resulted in child protective services showing up, who then, in conjunction with my parents, decided I needed to go to treatment. I remember thinking of the irony of these two-people sending me to treatment!

It was just one more thing to hold against my parents. Thirty days later, I was released into the care of my father. (Yes, they all knew what he had done and sent me there anyway.)

I did not return to school, nor did I have any intention to remain in Joe's company longer than it took to secure a ticket to freedom—a car in my own name paid for by Joe. I colored inside the lines for a short time, pretending to be the person he wanted me to be. Sure enough, he bought me another car. The ink was not even dry on the bill of sale before I was gone! Long story short, I jumped out of one fire and ran as fast as I could right into a four-alarm blaze.

His name was Shawn. He was twenty-one, good-looking, sexy and smooth-talking, and proclaimed his undying love and devotion to me. That was all it took to own my heart! He was also an abusive drunk and lived at the center of insanity. I cannot imagine why I would have attracted a guy like that! After a half-minute of dating, Shawn and I moved into a cheap three-room house on the wrong side of town. After several months of working two dead-end jobs (remember I was fifteen turning sixteen and paying for our apartment), abusing drugs and alcohol, and being abused, I once again turned to thoughts of suicide. This time my choices landed me in the custody of the state. My social worker sent me to the same treatment center I was in only a year earlier—only this time, I was a prisoner there.

After forty-five days, I realized they had no intentions of releasing me back into my old life, at least not any time soon, so I convinced a staff member to help me escape. Living on the run was harder than I thought.

I got into a fight that landed me in handcuffs. I was then sent to a locked-down facility for juvenile delinquents. I was court-ordered to remain there until my eighteenth birthday. I was not really feeling that vibe! Once again, I concocted an escape plan; one that required my father's help. My father picked me up about a mile outside the gates and took me to Albuquerque, New Mexico. He set me up in a hotel room and then returned to Kansas with the hope of securing my freedom from the state. I sat in that hotel room for what felt like an eternity. There are no words I can write that would paint an accurate picture of what it felt like to be so young, alone in a hotel many states away from home, hiding from the police, wondering if you will spend your next two birthdays incarcerated. What had my life become? Why was I here? What had I ever done that was so wrong, that I was deserving of this punishment? These were but a few of the questions consuming my thoughts. I was a failure, worthless, unworthy of love. I was deemed a criminal, yet I had committed no crimes. I'd become exactly who my family—my ecosystem—had positioned me to become. Why was this my fate? I was a child. How was any of this my fault? It was their crimes that had turned me into this person, yet it was not them running and hiding and hoping. Nothing made sense to me!

The day finally arrived that I had to appear before the judge. Somehow, I miraculously convinced him to emancipate me! I walked out of that courtroom free. But free was not even close to what I felt.

Days later, Shawn and I got back together and moved away. Thinking, I better start making some smarter choices, I went to the health clinic to get on birth control. *Oops!* Too *late*! I was sixteen, on my own, flat broke, and pregnant. At that moment, I knew my life was over and it was all my family's fault… But was it?

So, why have I shared this horrific two-year saga with you? I can assure it is not to elicit a sympathetic response. I have shared my ugly truth because this footer of accountability is so critically important to your joy. I wanted you to see how it only takes one domino to set off a chain reaction. No one ever said falling dominos had to lead to despair though. The chain reaction your dominos create is up to you! Accountability of choice is what will decide if your dominos fall right or fall left!

In January of 1988, my choice to drop out of school led to physical abuse, drug abuse, forced treatment, courts, fights, attempted suicide, a manhunt, jail, and an unplanned pregnancy.

I was only sixteen years old, and my life was a train wreck. It was two years of falling dominoes that could have been stopped had I made just one different choice. One choice caused back-to-back moments of impact that forever changed the trajectory of my life. I never got the chance to meet the woman that only now can I begin to imagine God intended I become! That, my friend, is what regret looks like! Regret is what I want to spare you.

There are two different types of accountability. There is accountability of choice and accountability of consequence. Most think in terms of the latter, but I want to challenge you to focus on your accountability of choice. True accountability is a commitment to the truth you are responsible for your choices, the steps of your journey, and the hustle you exert to get where you want to go. It is a commitment to being solely responsible for the outcome of each day you are given. How you choose to be accountable is a direct reflection of what you value and who you choose to be! People who value accountability—real accountability—claim full ownership for their choices, including the decision to act and the consequences for having done so. Accountable people do not apply action to thought until they are confident their desires are, aligned with their overall purpose, vision, mission, and values.

What do responsibility, ownership, choice, integrity, and values have in common? Each are required for accountability to exist.

I once heard a story about a woman called Joan. Joan had a good job, a home, and some money in the bank. She was a single mother of a young baby. When her baby was only a month old, she lost her job. Unable to pay her rent, she was soon evicted from her home. Joan spent every dime she had attempting to keep up with her bills. When her child was only seven months old, Joan and her baby were forced to live on the streets. As she had done many mornings before, Joan's baby woke crying with the pains of starvation. She could not stand another moment of hearing her child cry out in pain. She was willing to do anything to make sure her baby would not be hungry another minute.

Joan walked into the local grocery store feeling desperate and hopeless. She thought, *I only need a few cans of formula. No one will miss them or fault me for trying to feed my starving child!* There was a voice inside of her screaming, "Don't do it! If you get caught, you'll be arrested." But she talked herself into stealing anyway. She argued she had no other choice. Joan picked up the formula, looked around, placed them in her bag, and briskly walked toward the front door. The voices of discouragement were ringing in her head so loudly that she mistook them for store alarms. In a panic, Joan ran out of the store, activating actual alarms. When the police caught up to her, she pleaded with the officers to understand she had no other choice because her baby was starving. She begged the officer to understand how she had fallen on hard times and was not normally a thief.

The officer listened with great empathy before responding with these three questions. "Did you ask someone else to care for your baby until you got back on your feet?" Joan replied, "No, sir! I could not give my baby to someone else!" Next, he asked, "Did you seek the aid of a shelter for you and your child? There is one just up the road from here." Joan replied in frustration, "No, I could not take my child to a place like that?" Lastly, the officer asked, "Did you ask a single manager, clerk, or customer in the grocery store to buy food for your starving baby?" Joan hung her head and whispered, "No, sir! I could not ask anyone. They would have said I was a bad mother. They would have judged me."

The officer stood in silence for a moment and then looked at that tearful mother, dead straight in her eyes, and said, "Joan, I just presented you with three different choices you could have made—

ones that would not have resulted in your being in handcuffs, kissing your baby goodbye. There were many other paths you could have chosen. This is the one you decided to travel. You were accountable for the path you chose and now, you are accountable for the consequences of having done so."

Joan was held accountable to the consequences of her choices but failed in accepting accountability for the choice. Instead, she attempted to rationalize, justify, and blame her circumstances as things beyond her control. She used "lack of choice" as an excuse for her actions. She deflected the voice in her mind urging her not to steal. Joan claimed she valued her child above all else. But her actions revealed what Joan really valued was her pride.

Her circumstance would have changed had she accepted accountability before she made the choice to steal. If she truly valued her child and doing the right thing, she would have concluded that stealing the formula could lead to jail, and jail would lead to a separation from her child. She might have concluded that living on the street was alright for her but not was not for her child, and, therefore, sought interventions from family, friends, or systems. When she lost her job, she would have accepted her accountability of choice and resigned to working two or three part-time jobs if needed to maintain a home for her child. If Joan had accepted true accountability, then her values would have guided her choices. She would not have found herself in handcuffs, kissing her baby goodbye!

You are accountable for your choices. Until you get real with that truth, joy will always be elusive. You cannot live on purpose, with purpose, until you hold yourself accountable for your own circumstances. My family was not to blame for those last two years of hell, anymore than they were responsible for the hell I endured beyond that.

It was just easier to blame them than to accept the truth that my choices had created my ugly reality. I had a choice; I made the wrong ones because I didn't know how to be intentional or accountable.

Accountability is the third foundational footer for living a dare 2b more…life. If you are not willing to take ownership and responsibility for your choices, then you're essentially defining yourself as a person who values excuses, denial, deflection, and blame. You have given yourself permission to *not* dare 2b more...! Refusing accountability is choosing to settle for being an employee in the creation of your story.

I know what I believe to be true about accountability, but I wanted insight from another perspective. Naturally, I went to the leading authority on all things, Google! I conducted searches for accountable, accountability, the importance of each, why it matters, etc. The results bothered me tremendously because most of the information related to the workplace as if accountability were only relative to your work life. Much of the information equated being accountable as a tool to get ahead in your career. Countless others outlined accountability as being something another person forces upon you. While this certainly rings some truth, true accountability is the result of an intentional choice to honor your personal values and belief systems. Provided this statement is true, then at no point can another person *actually hold* you accountable!

Yes, I concede a person can task you with an assignment or outline expected behaviors and then render a consequence should you fail to perform accordingly, but that is not accountability of choice; it is accountability of consequence.

It comes down to this. We each have two choices in every situation we encounter: do the right thing or do not! For people who value accountability, doing what is right, will take precedence over the potential negative or positive consequences. They take ownership not only for making a choice but also for the outcomes, without blame or excuses. That is what accountability of choice looks like!

We are a people of sinful nature who screw up repeatedly. Doing the "right thing" may look different from your viewfinder than it does from mine. How can that be? Isn't it right and wrong, black and white? They should be but certainly are not. Right and wrong are dictated by what you intrinsically and non-negotiably value! This is why two people can look at the same situation and surmise something completely different.

I am a non-denominational Christian, through and through. That means my values are born in response to my faith. My perceptions of right and wrong are shaped and dictated by my faith. In Colossians 3, the scripture calls for us to rid ourselves of anger, rage, malice, slander, and filthy language. We are instructed to clothe ourselves with compassion, kindness, humility, gentleness, and patience. We are encouraged to bear with and forgive one another as the Lord has forgiven us and over all of these virtues put on love, which binds them together. In 1 Peter, we are commanded to use our gifts to serve others as faithful stewards of God's grace.

My values and the measure of the right and wrong to which I hold myself accountable include: compassion, humility, integrity, forgiveness, strong work ethic, accountability, and honor to name a few. My accountability of choice is guided by what I believe to be right and wrong, based on what I value. If I worked for an employer who instructed or insinuated that I perform any task that would undermine my integrity, I would decline even if doing so resulted in being terminated. My character belongs to me; it is not for sale, nor for another to choose. I am clear of my values, purpose, and ultimately to whom I am accountable. I am unwilling to compromise my integrity for a paycheck; to do so would create a series of negative consequences that would undoubtedly steal my joy.

You are the COO of InJOYou, Inc. You are accountable for the product your business turns out. You cannot build InJOYou, Inc., or live a dare 2b more…life until you first define with complete certainty what your values are.

Once you have done that, then your choices can be guided by those values. Your barometer of right and wrong will be clear. Then and only then will you become an excuseless person who does not blame another for your plot in life. When you decide to eliminate permissions to blame others, make excuses, deflect truth, and deny yourself accountability and responsibility for your circumstances, you will be genuinely accountable. When you own your accountability of choice, you can get off the hamster wheel and start building your most joy-filled life.

What accountability do you need to own today for your current circumstance? What are the excuses that are granting you permission to remain stuck? What could change in your life right now if you stopped blaming, stopped making excuses, and started being accountable?

DARE 2B MORE… BE ACCOUNTABLE.

DARE 2B MORE… InJOYou.com

Chapter 10

Footer 4—Dream

He said, "Listen to my words: When there is a prophet among you, I, the Lord, reveal myself to them in visions, I speak to them in dreams."
—Numbers 12:6 (NIV)

The very substance of the ambitious is merely the shadow of a dream.
—William Shakespeare

Growing up, I was surrounded by people who did not dream. They did not think beyond the moment in front of them. I can't recall a single person who encouraged my imagination, let alone interjected hope into my dreams. Thinking back, it's entirely possible that I was the only person who did dare to dream beyond the realities. As you can imagine, that kind of an ecosystem creates a huge problem for an inquisitive child.

Although the players in my ecosystem were not dreamers or even goals setters…for whatever reason, I was! My imagination allowed me to escape the misery of my reality. I took wildly adventurous trips, built great empires, flew jets, and invented the next "big thing." Traveling through my magical daydreams filled my soul with a sense of peace and joy. They gave me hope! On occasion, I would get so excited about some new idea that amnesia would set in, allowing my heart to flow like water. But just as one would regret plummeting over a one-hundred-foot waterfall without so much as a life jacket, such was the regret I felt each time I shared my lofty ideas with any other person in my ecosystem. My village capsized every idea as fast as a sailboat in a hurricane, leaving me feeling stupid and embarrassed. There certainly was not a shortage of dream killers living in my village!

My first real dream came when my grandfather and mom took my younger cousin and me to visit the Naval Academy in Annapolis, Maryland. I was eleven years old. I had a deep affection for naval pilots—naturally spurred by the fact that several family members were once naval aviators.

I remember walking across that campus, enamored by the men and women in white. My grandfather explained to us these students were the "cream of the crop, the best of the best." They would go on to become officers in the United States Navy. Something inside of me stirred; I saw myself in their likeness. I imagined putting on flight gear, climbing into the cockpit, and saluting just before I blazed upward into the highest clouds, ready to defend our freedoms. My daydream felt so amazing; piloting navy jets was my destiny.

I snapped back to reality after being reminded that my falling behind was holding up the show. I did not care that my mother was annoyed; I had a dream; I wanted to proclaim it to the heavens! I proclaimed with great exuberance, "When I grow-up, I'm going to attend the naval academy and become a fighter pilot!" They all looked at me somewhat bewildered and in unison started to chuckle. My grandfather eagerly educated me of the reasons why a dream of this magnitude was impossible for someone "like me." He reminded me that I was ignorant and lacked the scholarly demeanor required to pursue that kind of a dream. I laughed it off with some flippant retort, but secretly, I was devastated that my own family thought so little of my competencies.

After that trip, I stopped dreaming aloud and eventually stopped believing in the delusion that I would ever be a "somebody"! I replaced those childhood dreams with other things, things that allowed me to become exactly who my family had deemed I would be—nothing!

I never stopped dreaming; I just stopped believing they would ever be my reality. As a child, I dreamed in first person, but as I grew older, more cynical, and more aware of my inadequacies, I stopped dreaming in first person and started to dream in third. That was the only way my dreams could live on without bearing the disappointment of failure.

Unbeknownst to me, there was a silver lining in those dream-crushing moments of my childhood. They fueled a determination to do what I wanted, even if what I wanted was not so great for me in the long run! I adopted this belief system that both saved and destroyed my life. It was the belief the impossible was possible! Anytime I heard the words "No" or "You can't," I understood them to mean you have permission to keep going. Admittedly, to this day, when I see a "No Trespassing" sign, I have to remind myself it's not an invitation!

As a teen, that attitude found more trouble than praise. As I became more of the person I truly wanted to be, and time and space severed my family's cult-like control, that belief system was the very thing—the only thing—that allowed me to step up and overcome the seemingly impossible. There was, however, one small caveat. There was little I could not achieve or overcome if I believed that another's happiness depended on my performance.

The voices of my past haunted me! They echoed in my mind like cymbals clanging over the Grand Canyon. *You foolish woman! You are not competent or worthy to have or realize your own dreams.* I made it my mission to help others realize their dreams rather than be disappointed by the failing of my own. My heart and soul, time and talents, and strengths and tools worked in perfect harmony to turn every "No" into a "Yes" as long as it meant another person would know happiness.

Your dreams are the heartbeat of everything you want to achieve. The dreams God has placed on your heart are meant to be realized. Please believe me when I tell you, if others are killing your dreams, it's not because of who you are or what you can achieve; it's because they've lost the ability to dream. They've lost hope and replaced it with fear, so don't you listen to them! When others diminish your capacity or assign failure to you, it speaks to their limitations, not yours—unless you choose to let small-minded people define your beliefs about who you are and what you can achieve. That choice is your accountability.

What you need to know is God does not give you dreams (that are of his design) without also providing everything you need to bring them to fruition. What God does not do is make you move. That is a choice he placed in your hands when he gifted you with free will. However, don't be fooled; God's will will not be thwarted regardless of the choices you or I make. God has a way of disrupting our trajectory if we remain insistent upon choosing the wrong path.

Think back to when you were a child. Remember how you once let your dreams play out in your imagination freely and wildly without inhibition or boundary? Of what did you dream? Where did your imagination take you? What did you imagine your future would be? Pause for just a moment. Close your eyes; drift back to a time when you allowed your dreams to run wild. What do you see? Your dreams became realities in the stories you made up, the games you played, the toys you brought to life, and in the costumes you sported with immeasurable pride and confidence.

Perhaps this is why small children are so inspiring to adults; they lack inhibitions or fear of failing. Children believe the dreams of today, are the realities of tomorrow. The spirit of a child, the freeness of their imagination, is the same spirit you must rejuvenate to live a dare 2b more…life. The difference between the person who dreams of doing, seeing, experiencing, and the one who has done, seen, and experienced is twenty seconds of courage to go-all-in! Courage is not fearlessly moving ahead, but rather a choice, and a decision to try, while still, fully afraid. It is your dreams that lead to your goals. Dreams are the vision for the direction of your life. Without dreams, your journey becomes a series of days and nights that lack energy, passion, and purpose! Without a dream to pursue, your heart and soul are like a car with a dead battery—fully functional on the outside but dysfunctional on the inside. This leads to your feeling stuck, hopeless, and eventually filled with more regrets than joy.

For individuals born into an unhealthy ecosystem—as I was—or who live void of an encouraging, supportive network, dreaming can feel like a useless waste of time and energy. Have you adopted the mindset of "What is the point in dreaming?" If you have, let that lie go right now! Instead, start asking yourself a new question, "What is the cost of *not* dreaming?" When what you dream of is surviving the day, paying the bills, feeding your children, keeping a job or getting one, or just getting the kids to soccer on time, there seems to be little room left for the big dreams—the kind that create a pivot in your circumstance. I'm here to tell you that one big dream you are denying yourself has the power to change everything in your field of vision.

I have talked with countless people who have adopted the mindset that dreaming is a luxury they cannot afford. They have convinced themselves dreams are reserved for the privileged, for the rich, and for the other guy! If I could change one single thing with the wave of a magical wand, it would be to eradicate any and all inhibitions killing your ability to dream big, bold, and beautiful dreams—even those that feel impossible. Hope lives in your ability to dream! Dreams create and hold the space for you to hope—to have faith—and believe in what is possible!

Without hope, there is no faith! Without faith, there is no hope! Faith and hope are what drive you forward—they are the vehicles that will make your dreams come true! To intrinsically believe the impossible is possible, you must intentionally weave hope and faith into your dreams!

Dream Big! Dream Bold!

I borrowed the following quotes, accompanied by clarifications, from an article written by Jayson DeMers. This compilation of inspirational quotes speaks to the truth that dreaming is the beginning of each new chapter!

You have to dream before your dreams can come true.
—A. P. J. Abdul Kalam

Some people throttle their potential by refusing to think "what if?" and ignoring what is truly important to them in life. You have to start dreaming before you can achieve anything.

To be a human being is to be in a state of tension between your appetites and your dreams, and the social realities around you and your obligations to your fellow man.
—John Updike

Our dreams are often at odds with our realities, demanding freedoms and resources we may not have. But this does not make them impossible to achieve.

Once in a while it really hits people that they don't have to experience the world in the way they have been told.
—Alan Keightley

This is the realization that fuels most people to follow their dreams relentlessly. Staying complacent never led anybody to greatness.

> *It is better to risk starving to death than surrender.*
> *If you give up on your dreams, what's left?*
> —Jim Carrey

> *This quote may be a bit extreme, but it carries*
> *a great point; your dreams define you.*
> *If you abandon them, what else could possibly motivate you?*

Dream your butt off! If you are going to dream, then *dare* to *dream huge*, *bold*, and *fiercely awesome* dreams. I would almost challenge you to abandon the wimpy, small dreams in exchange for the wildly challenging ones. Trust me when I say that if people are not doubting you, questioning your ideas of what is possible, or challenging your boldness to achieve your dreams, then you are not really tapping into all the possibilities for your future. Allow yourself the freedom to tap into that child's voice inside you and let go of every fear, doubt, worry, and realism, stamping your dreams DOA (dead on arrival). Leave that suitcase of lies out on the curb for the trashmen to take away. Start dreaming of what you could achieve, if only you were willing to take one…single step…forward! The awesomeness of starting from a seemingly impossible place is that you will bring countless smaller dreams and goals to fruition along the way. Before too long what seemed impossible will look and feel entirely possible.

Your dreams must have teeth to bite! In other words, your dreams must be so clear, so real, and so inspiring you will not allow the roadblocks to stop you in your tracks when things get hard. I came up with two acronyms to help me remember what the word *dream* and *hard* actually mean.

DREAM = *Do* the work | *Remember* your why | *Effort* = Results | *Accountability* is key | *Mentors* know the way

HARD = *Heighten* your *Attention* to *Resources* available and be *Disciplined*

Christopher Reeve, America's Superman, is the absolute best example of a person who dreamed an impossible dream. He dreamed boldly—rejecting the voices of doubt, realism, difficulty, and "medical certainty." He dared "impossible" to stand in his way of walking just one more time.

In 1995, Superman was paralyzed from the neck down following a horse-riding accident. Although America's beloved Superman passed away before fully realizing his dream to walk again, he did bring about many smaller dreams others said were impossible to achieve.

As quoted in the Baltimore Sun:

> *Dr. John McDonald of Washington University in St. Louis, who designed the exercise program, said that, in the past year, Reeve could move his legs on a recumbent bicycle without help from machines. "Chris was the worst case; he had no functional recovery for five years and his injury was as severe as it gets," said McDonald, who spoke with Reeve a few weeks ago. "He went on to recover sensation throughout his entire body, and after a few years he could move the muscles in his arms, legs and abdomen. Any recovery would have been substantial," McDonald said. "But Chris achieved about 20 percent functional improvement, which is amazing."*

What if Superman dreamed only to feel again anywhere below his neck? Do you think he would have worked as hard? Do you think he would have pushed the envelope, challenged the medical community, and searched for each and every path of possibility to walk again? Do you think he would have felt the same sense of urgency?

It does not matter that his wildly huge dream did not come to fruition as he hoped. What mattered was he made a choice, sitting in his wheelchair, completely paralyzed—unable to be the Superman he had always been—*to live on purpose, with purpose*, each and every day of his life without excuse! He was faithful, forgiving, accountable, intentional, and dared to dream wildly, bold dreams! He dared 2b more…and in doing so, took the rest of the world on his journey of inspiration and hope! Christopher Reeves defied the predictions made by medical experts because he had faith that could move mountains, and the courage to dream beyond what others defined as possible. If he can do that, imagine what you can achieve.

Never forget, that while pursuing your huge, wildly bold dreams, smaller dreams are brought to fruition. You must know where you are going before you can map the route to get there!

Today, right now, in this exact minute, you can dare 2b more... What dreams have you given up? What dreams have you ignored? What dreams have you let the voices of doubt silence? What dream is fear stealing from you today?

DARE 2B MORE... BE DREAMFUL.

DARE 2B MORE… InJOYou.com

Chapter 11

Footer 5—Intentional Choice

Who is wise and understanding among you? Let them show it by their good life, by deeds done in the humility that comes from wisdom.
—James 3:13

But the wisdom that comes from heaven is first of all pure; then peace-loving, considerate, submissive, full of mercy and good fruit, impartial and sincere.
—James 3:17

I find that mindfully taking a moment to ritualize my intentions helps me to will that best, most exalted self into being.
—Mya Spalter

The secret to custom designing a life that is sustained by joy is...*intentional choice!*

Have you ever asked yourself, "Is this as good as it gets? Is this all there is? Am I meant for more?" Those were the exact questions I felt haunted by in January of 2018.

I lived in Maryland for thirty years. If I am being honest, I detested all thirty years of it! Of course, there were things that were familiar and places I enjoyed and people I loved. I had a few close friends although I rarely saw them. Deep down, the weather, politics, pace, corporate culture, geographical location, traffic, and the fleeting presence of God, were never-ending tolls on my soul. I felt restless and anxious and constantly annoyed! The things I most enjoyed were not easily accessible, and I felt as if my life was little more than a to-do list.

Also true was that for my children—the keepers of my whole heart—Maryland was home. Their dad, siblings, cousins, and grandparents reside in Maryland. Everyone I loved had deep roots in a place, that for me, never felt like home. I forced myself to adopt the ideology that *life is not where you are, but what you make of it.* All the people with whom I wanted to do life called Maryland home. Doing life with them meant I had to live there as well. I convinced myself that I did not have a choice. The truth was I did have a choice, but the cost of making the right choice for me was just too great! Leaving Maryland was in direct conflict with my values, and I knew it! So, for thirty years, I chose my family's joy above my own. I adapted! But… the reasons I adapted to life in Maryland were sprouting their wings to attend college nine hundred miles away from home.

My entire purpose and reason for being—my children—were about to embark on a new journey. It was a journey that did not include me, at least not in the way it once had. I did not know how to do everyday life without the constant presence of my children. I did not know how to be anything more than their mom! What I did know was that I did not want to do life in Maryland without them. It was time for a change! It was time to build my life's business—that of InJOYou, Inc.

Earlier on in this book, I talked about how ecosystems are designed to support the growth of some while restricting or inhibiting it for others. (Remember the alligator and the butterflies.) Maryland was the wrong ecosystem for my growth and joy. To successfully live in that ecosystem, I had to adapt. Adapting was a choice, but the truth was for thirty years, I tried to grow in an ecosystem not designed to support the growth or joy I most desired.

The ecosystem I believed could best support the life I wanted existed in North Carolina! Nowhere else I'd experienced felt more like home! Quite intentionally, I chose a small town just outside of Charlotte to build my business of InJOYou, Inc. It checked all the boxes needed to support, grow, and sustain my joy. But…moving came at a cost, a huge cost.

Moving meant disrupting my children's ecosystem—their parents would be in two separate states—and the one parent (me) they had always lived with would no longer call their hometown home. Leaving Maryland meant leaving my adult children, grandson, the love of my life, the friends I called family, and the career I'd built from the ground up. Taking this journey meant I would walk alone—completely alone. As if those factors were not significant enough, there was also the matter of financing this new life I wanted. I had been self-employed for over twenty years. Moving meant quite literally starting over as a single woman for the very first time in my life, in a strange town and state, without a home, job, friends, family, or connections. (Well, that is not entirely true. I do have an aunt and uncle in the area who allowed me to stay with them for three weeks, but beyond that, I was 100 percent on my own.) Not one of those barriers mattered a single bit to me. I was sick and tired of being sick and tired. I was willing to sacrifice everything, to stare down my fears and take a huge leap of faith for the opportunity to build a life of sustainable joy—the kind of life that I finally believed was possible for someone like me.

My loved ones vehemently pointed out that I was an idiot, selfish, and thoughtless just for dreaming of moving, let alone doing it. Talk about making hard choices! I felt incredibly selfish and inconsiderate. I was making a choice that would negatively impact those I loved most. I was riddled with guilt, fear, and anxiety. These were certainly not the feelings a person chasing her, quote unquote, "perfect life" ought to feel.

Further complicating the situation was the reality that I was a forty-six-year-old woman who earned my living as a professional photographer. Do you know how little most photographers get paid, let alone how crowded the playing field is? It had taken me nearly ten years to build a successful and thriving portrait studio in an area where I knew people and had a referral business. I reached the status of being one of the top senior portrait photographers in my area. I was teaching and mentoring high school students and other women; both were roles I deeply cherished. What was I doing? How was I going to do this? I was headed to nothing and leaving everything. I dropped to my knees and prayed, "Jesus, am I making the right choice? Is this really what you want me to do? I'm so afraid I will fail. Please give me the strength and courage to go; let me know that I am honoring your will, not my own."

I bet you are kind of curious as to why I would intentionally disrupt my life in such a dramatic manner. Two reasons: (1) This was the call God placed on my heart. When God calls, I say, "Yes!" (2) Life is precious and fleeting; living a joy-filled life should not be optional. I invested forty-six years into creating and existing in an ecosystem consumed with pain; my emotional bank account was bankrupt!

The time had come to choose a path—stay for them or leave for me. Not once in my life had I considered my well-being before that of another. Was I selfish? What if I was wrong? What if moving led to more pain and suffering? Was it right to want to claim joy for me if it meant causing heartache to the people I had willingly and gladly sacrificed the entirety of my soul to honor, love, and protect? I was a broken woman with nothing left to give them. I knew, deep down, that what was right for me was wrong for my children, but I could not continue to pour from an empty cup. Though my heart was overwhelmed and burdened, I weighed each option, prayed, waited for guidance—for permission to be, finally freed.

Intentional choices are guided by values and rooted with clearly defined "whys." I knew my purpose—*joy*. My vision was clear—build and leave a legacy of *joy*. My values were and are etched in stone. I had defined the ecosystem that could best support, grow, and sustain my joy in the storms, as well as would allow me to use my gifts and talents to manufacture and distribute a product of joy. My mission was clear. I had done the work; it was now time to breathe life into my Eco-Print.

Once I made the decision to move forward with constructing InJOYou, Inc., it only took eight months to complete. October 3, 2018, with the gut-wrenching goodbyes said, my belongings packed, loaded, and stored, I began a faith-inspired journey to reclaim my superpower of intentional choice. As I looked into the rearview mirror, watching my old life slowly fade away, I could not restrict the endless stream of tears flowing from faucets of doubt and fear buried deeply within. At the same time, I felt this sense of excitement and empowerment begging to be acknowledged. With each passing mile, I felt the chains holding my joy hostage break link by link, but as they did, so did my heart! Many a mile I'd traveled before that day but never before with fear and joy battling for authority. Joy would persevere! It was a faith-filled certainty!

Today, my life is sustained by joy! This is not to say everything has been roses. This journey was not easy; the challenges have been and are many. The greatest difference is that now when the storms roll in, I do not feel a need to run for cover! I am good right where I am because I am doing life in an ecosystem that I custom-designed to support my joy with great care and intention! For the first time, I have a surplus of joy to share with those I love, care for, and for the many who will come and go as I travel across this grand adventure called life. Gone are the days of walking in the shadows of darkness broken, alone, and emotionally bankrupt. Living joy-filled is no longer optional; each day I am given I make the choice to live free and joy-filled. Today, I am authentically and non-negotiably me! Nothing feels better than giving yourself the gift of joy and knowing that because you did, all those you hold so dear are receiving the very best of you!

I once knew an exceptionally sage man who shared this piece of wisdom with me. He said, *"Darling, to each of us is given a box of tools and a book of rules, with which some will build stumbling blocks, while others stepping stools. Choose wisely how you use your tools!"*

Your greatest tool is that of *free will*! Only you can decide if you will use your *free will* to build stumbling blocks or stepping stools. Stepping stools are the result of making intentional choices! A dare 2b more…life is guided by faith, defined by non-negotiable and flexible values alike, and steered by intentional choices. What is an intentional choice? It honors your purpose, vision, mission, and values! Intentional choices are not reckless, selfish, self-centered, narcissistic, or void of consideration for the impact on others' joy and happiness.

Your toolbox is fully equipped with all you need to build a grand staircase leading anywhere you desire. You are enough! You are gifted and talented and beautiful and special! You are a superhero with the superpower of choice! You were created to give and to receive joy! The only thing standing between you and the life you want (between who you are now and who you most want to be) are your choices! Don't you think it is about time to start making choices purposed to grow your joy rather than steal it? If your answer is yes, then start making *intentional choices*!

There is a huge distinction between making a choice and making an intentional choice. A choice is one made without giving consideration to accountability, consequence, purpose, mission, vision, or most importantly, values! An intentional choice is one that demands answers to questions before your thoughts are coupled with action.

Have you ever given consideration for the wonderment of opening your eyes? You wake each day not because you commanded your eyes to open or your heart to beat, but because your creator, as I believe God, allowed you another day. Beyond the moment of your eyes opening, God steps back and allows you to choose how you will spend each and every minute right up until you close your eyes again that night. When sleep overcomes you, God takes back the wheel and either grants you a new dawn or brings you home. I am truly baffled by those without faith. Not one person can control the opening of our eyes once they have closed!

What is more amazing to me are the number of people who disregard the gift of waking up, of being granted a superpower of such immeasurable force—as though it were something ordinary or insignificant or merely scientific. Really? My point is this: You do not know the minutes, hours, days, months, or years that remain in your life account; time is not yours to deposit—not even a second of more time is within your control. So why then would you spend the minutes you are gifted in the spirit of pain, suffering, misery, anxiety, or the like, *on purpose*, when you have the superpower of intentional choice at your disposal?

Let me give some clarity to this superpower of yours. Your superpower is *not* the ability to make a "choice." Your *superpower* is the ability to make an *intentional* choice. You can literally choose to custom design an ecosystem that can sustain the joy you want and were created to experience. The power is yours! You can step into it anytime you choose, or you can ignore it and continue to live reactively, constantly blaming, making excuses, or being paralyzed by fear.

Unfortunately, there is another truth about free will and choice that most conveniently reject—your choices yield consequences! (This should be a no-brainer, but for some reason it is not.) Choice and consequence work in tandem…*always*! This is the trade-off for your *free will*. It is also the reason you need to be clear about who granted your superpower in the first place. Often the choices before you won't be comfortable, easy, or void of sacrifice, but make no mistake; you always have a choice. We have each experienced those moments when it feels like there is no choice. You know those moments when no matter which way you turn, someone will be hurt. Most people love to overlook this fact: by not making a choice, you, in fact, are making a choice. You choose to stay the course and resign to living unfulfilled with heartache, pain, anxiety, frustration, and regrets. Why would some choose to live unfulfilled when they can live joy-filled? Having been there, I know the answer is simple—it's easier! After a while, the toxic stuff is the only stuff that feels easy to navigate, digest, and predict. Sometimes the bad stuff is just easier to believe. People don't change the things they are fully in control of changing because the unfamiliar is scary. But do not lie to yourself; do not pretend that there are no options available to you. You are in control of your free will; your path is for you to choose, and just like Joan—the single mom you learned about earlier—you are accountable for the choices you make and for the ones you don't.

Whether you choose to take a step back, stand still, or step forward, you are making a decision for your life, not merely for a single situation. (If you disagree, refer back to my single decision to cut school one day.) *Free will* is not a gift that entitles you to "have it all" nor will it save you from the hardships or the pains of this life. That is a lie.

We all begin from the same starting point—birth! We all arrive at the same destination—death! What is different are the choices we make in between. You are not in control of another anymore than they are in control of you, regardless of those who think the contrary! This is why bad things happen to good people! Rarely accepted is the truth that every generation is subject to the consequences of choices made by those prior—a fact that dates back to Adam and Eve, the first created in the image of God.

Our *free will* is what causes bad crap to happen, not God! We pollute our waters and lands, filling them with chemicals and toxins. The animals and vegetation absorb those chemicals, and then we absorb them as food. And we wonder why illness exists! We blame God when our loved ones fall ill…but it was not God who polluted the Earth; it was you and I and every generation before us! God gave us a perfect land with only one instruction—do not eat the apple! If you do, bad stuff will happen! Apparently, that was too much to ask! My grandmother used to describe my friends of questionable character as "bad apples." Now I understand the analogy!

The world distorts the meaning of *free will*. The world fails to make it clear that while you are free to choose, you are also bound by the consequences of your choice. Everything in your ecosystem will bear those consequences—both the good and bad. Your choices create a ripple effect. (Think of the pebble in the still pond or the unseen shifting of the earth's tectonic plates that cause tsunamis in the oceans.)

Free will is a power meant to be exerted with great care and intention, guided by godly values, and bound together by an understanding that every action has a subsequent reaction for you and those you do life with. We are human beings full of thoughts, wants, and needs. But not everything we want is good for us! You need to question your choices *before* you take action! The beauty and benefit of questions are they demand an answer. It is your answers that will dictate the quality of the products that InJOYou, Inc., can and will produce! The next time you are confronted with anything, literally, anything that impacts your life, from eating a candy bar to getting married, to how you live your life, pause and ask of your choices a few of these questions.

Is what I want going to move me closer or further from my purpose, mission and vision, and joy? Is this going to grow or steal joy—God's, others', and my own? Is what I want in line with my values—specifically those that are non-negotiable? Am I willing to pay the cost to have what I want (the cost of your time, treasure, talent, loss, relationships, status, reputation, respect, freedom, risk, etc.)? Will what I want bring harm to myself or another? Is that harm something I can accept?

When you demand your desires be intentionally vetted before they can be acted upon, the right choices—the ones that will manufacture and distribute joy—become undeniably clear and simple to navigate. (Notice I did not say easy; I said simple.)

In no way am I implying that by merely making intentional choices, you will be spared sorrow or heartache or pain. Intentional choices lead you down paths that honor your values, mission, vision, and purpose. When you commit to making intentional choices—to respond rather than react—the good and right answers will become crystal clear.

Footer 5, intentional choice, is not meant to confirm you have a choice. Let us be real; that is a no-brainer! A toddler knows he has a choice! This footer is designed for those who want to create a life of less regret, pain, anxiety, restlessness, and despair. Intentional choice is for those who are not willing to settle for anything less than to build, live, and leave a legacy of joy for all whom your light touches!

Remember the story of the single mom I shared with you earlier—the homeless mom who shoplifted the formula to feed her baby? Joan reacted to her circumstance rather than responding to it. She made a choice, but she did not make an intentional choice. She asked the question: What do I want? Her answer was "I want to feed my baby now!" Sadly, that was not really what she wanted even though it was what she wanted at that exact moment! If we break it down, Joan's purpose was joy—a life free of pain—for her child. Her vision was to create a life of provision, security, and care for her family. Her mission was to build a life that would ensure they never were hungry again. She believed her values included integrity and love. The problem was Joan was not clear of her purpose, mission, vision, or values. As cruel as this may sound to some, at its core, her choice was selfish and had less to do with her baby than we would like to believe.

She made a choice that put her need to ease her own pain above her desire to feed her baby. She put her pride and her fear of judgment and failure in front of doing the right thing. Her behavior reflected that what she truly valued was her own pride. Regardless of her circumstances or our empathy for the circumstances that led to her choice, the fact remains she did have a choice in who she chose to be and how she chose to respond. *(You can tell me who you are, but I'll know by what you show me! When someone shows you who they are, believe them!)*

What if Joan would have paused long enough to question her intended actions, allowing her the space to make an intentional choice rather than just a choice?

What if she asked of her desire: Will this yield the result I really want? *No! It could land me in jail which would separate me from my baby.* Will my choice to steal honor my values and my purpose? *No, I am an honest person. I could be convicted of theft. That could prevent me from being hired in a position that would allow me to create the life of provision I want for my baby.* Am I willing to pay the price for my choice to steal? Am I willing to possibly lose my baby or my freedom, or to be branded as a thief, spend time in jail, do community service, or pay fines? Am I willing to lose the respect of my family and friends, or to create challenges in obtaining gainful employment to alleviate the pain of this moment? If there were another option, what would it be?

If Joan accepted her superpower to make intentional choices, she would have come to the conclusion that stealing might feed her baby right now, but it might also prevent her from being able to feed her baby tomorrow, which was what she really wanted!

To summarize, you always have a choice; you may not like the choices you have, but make no mistake about it, you do have a choice! You can make choices in your life that react to your circumstances, or you can make intentional choices that respond to your circumstances.

The "choice" is yours!

DARE 2B MORE… BE INTENTIONAL.

DARE 2B MORE... InJOYou.com

Chapter 12

Footer 6—Acceptance

"For I know the plans I have for you," declares the Lord, "plans to prosper you and not to harm you, plans to give you hope and a future.
—Jeremiah 29:11

Your present circumstances don't determine where you can go; they merely determine where you start.—Nido Qubein

Acceptance from my personal perspective can be summed up in two sentences: Life happens! What are you going to do about it?

I once knew this great couple, Bobby and Sue, who created a truly fabulous life together! Both had exciting and lucrative careers they loved, a gorgeous home in the perfect location, and a network of close family and friends with whom they shared life. They were longstanding, active members of their church and were deeply rooted in faith! Everyday life for them included all the things that fed their joy, both individually and as a couple. Bobby and Sue had done everything they could to build a life sustained by joy. They felt blessed beyond measure.

One day, while driving home from work, a deer came out of nowhere, forcing Bobby to swerve off the road at 55 mph to avoid striking the dear head-on. His car flipped numerous times before slamming into a tree and finally coming to rest at the bottom of a ravine.

Bobby suffered numerous injuries and required months of intensive inpatient care, followed by several more months of rehabilitative therapy. A few weeks after Bobby's accident, a hurricane ravaged their seaside town, causing massive damage to their home and displacing Sue. (Bobby was still in the rehabilitation center.) Only a week later, Sue's company merged with another, causing massive layoffs, including to Sue's position. Bobby became increasingly enraged by all that was happening to his family and the life they knew only a few weeks ago.

He wanted to be positive and tried to lean into his faith, but at the end of the day, depression was overtaking his resolve to remain either positive or faithful. Bobby was truly struggling to see any existence of a silver lining. He could no longer physically be the provider and the source of strength on which his wife had always depended. He felt helpless, hopeless, worthless, and deeply resentful! Soon he stopped praying, denied visits from his friends or family, and started arguing with Sue about everything. (Something they had never done before.) Physical therapy yielded a sum of pain that Bobby could not bear. Frustrated and overcome by suffering, Bobby stopped giving his all. His diminished will to persevere lengthened his road to recovery. He was so focused on what had gone wrong that his entire mindset shifted from hope and faith and optimism to one of bitterness and resignation. Watching her husband spiral downward left Sue feeling desperate to restore the life they once had. But how?

Sue made a commitment to herself to dare 2b more...to Dare 2B faithful, forgiving, dream-filled, accountable, and intentional!

Sue knew that they had built InJOYou, Inc., atop a foundation reinforced by footers so deep and wide, it could withstand the battering winds and rains from the fiercest of storms.

Immediately following Bobby's accident, she rallied her community together to pray for her husband's healing. She thanked God with gratitude that Bobby had not died nor was he paralyzed, as the perplexed doctors repeated, he ought to be. Determined to help her husband, Sue sought every piece of information she could find relative to his injuries. Upon discovering a relatively new and cutting-edge therapeutic, she presented her findings to Bobby's lead physician, who immediately incorporated the methodologies into Bobby's treatment plan. This course of action reduced his recovery time by half that previously anticipated. Sue read that the demands of being a caretaker could be brutal, so she immediately located and joined a support group that she could lean on in her moments of weakness. In her support group, she met an insurance agent and a real estate agent. Ironically, Bobby's accident had caused Sue to reevaluate all their insurance policies. The agent she met in the support group helped Sue to secure a much better homeowner's policy, just two weeks before the storm hit. The new policy included a hurricane rider—one the previous policy had not!

And what of that real estate agent? It turns out she had a vacant furnished rental, which she gladly offered to Sue until the contractors could repair their home. While visiting her husband, she ran into an old friend who told her of a position that was opening up—one for which Sue would be perfect. She was able to apply for it and secure the position before it was even released to the public. Each day, Sue was resolute to remain faithful, forgiving, accountable, intentional, and…accepting.

Bobby had always been the main provider for their family, the primary decision maker, and her greatest encourager. Sue felt completely unprepared and inadequate to step into her husband's shoes. Both she and Bobby understood that they had to accept what had come to be their new normal. However, there was a pivotal difference in their understanding of what that acceptance looked like. For Bobby, acceptance meant, *it is what it is*! He understood acceptance to mean resignation! But for Sue, acceptance meant, *it is what it is; now what am I going to do about it?* She understood that acceptance did not mean resignation but rather a call, a challenge, a directive to adjust their sails! She didn't cancel the vision she and Bobby were working toward; she accepted that a detour had popped up and so adjusted the route and kept moving forward.

She looked for the opportunities to dare 2b more…and then approached the situation from the perspective that everything on earth is temporary. Sue accepted what was real; their lives and plans had changed. But then she challenged that reality by asking only one question: What am I going to do about it? The first thing she did was to check her foundational footers for signs of potential stress cracks.

Bobby forgot about the foundational footers. He allowed stress cracks to grow, and as a result, his footers crumbled in the storm. He lost faith, held on to his anger and resentments, forgot that he was accountable, stopped dreaming of a better tomorrow, relinquished his superpower of intentional choice, and failed in his understanding of acceptance. He was so blinded by his negative perspective that he could not see the abundance of blessings that were showing up in the midst of the storm! He could not see that God had not abandoned them but was providing them with the people, places, and things that could restore them. Bobby chose to trade his position as the COO of InJOYou, Inc., for that of an employee. He chose to react rather than respond. By doing so, he gave pain the opportunity to replace joy as his CEO.

There are two schools of thought relative to the meaning of acceptance as it relates to one's circumstance.

The first school of thought says, "*Accept* what is, is! Let go of everything else!" In other words, *grow where you're planted; keep the wheel turning!*

Think of the farmer whose son, grandson, and great-grandson also become farmers because of an ingrained belief system that, *farming is what we do*. The conversation might go like this: Dad: "Get on the tractor!" Son: "But I don't want to be a farmer?" Dad: "I don't care! Your place is here on the farm helping your family." Son: "Okay, Dad, it is what it is! I guess I do not have a choice!"

The second school of thought holds a worldview that believes life is happening for them, not to them! They see setbacks, failures, and disappointments as opportunities to learn, pivot, and grow! The person who elects this point of view acknowledges the reality of what is now but then accepts they are accountable for preventing any joy-stealing weeds from taking root in their ecosystem. Thus, they continue to walk forward, pivot when needed, abandon the toxic, and persistently work to overcome or change the things they can. They lean into their foundational footers and refuse to resign to living a life that is uncomfortably, comfortable simply because it's easier to do so!

Before you can build, let alone live a dare 2b more…life, you need to understand that sometimes, regardless of your best efforts, things aren't going to go as you imagined, planned, or hoped. Things beyond your control will emerge; it is not a matter of if, but when. Another truth is that sometimes what you want is not in line with what God wants for you or from you. What you want just might not be good for you. When life throws you a curveball, rather than feeling sorry for yourself—getting mad, down, resentful, or quitting—ask a question: What can I do, think, say, or feel right now to change the situation threatening to steal my joy? What do I have control over in this circumstance?

Accepting your current reality does not mean resigning to a belief that tomorrow will undoubtedly be, just more of the same. You are not a hamster nor are you meant to be an employee in your story; you can get off the wheel anytime you want!

When you view life as happening for you, rather than to you, you will suddenly notice that countless opportunities arise for you to pivot, often in the least and most unexpected ways. But for that to happen, you must be ready and open to receive and recognize them as such!

> *"There is a wonderful old Italian joke about a poor man who goes to church every day and prays before the statue of a great saint, begging, 'Dear saint-please, please, please…give me the grace to win the lottery.' This lament goes on for months. Finally, the exasperated statue comes to life, looks down at the begging man, and says in weary disgust, 'My son please, please, please…buy a ticket'"* (Elizabeth Gilbert, Eat, Pray, Love).

Often, you get stuck in the same place, wishing in one hand and wanting in the other—too blinded by circumstance to realize that everything would change if only you would pivot, just a single step, to the right or left. I once heard a speaker say, "Be careful what you define as hell because things can always get worse." How many times have you thought, things just can't get any worse, then they do? You have the ability to overcome. How you respond to your circumstances when things do not go your way is what will define you and your journey. How you interpret the meaning of *acceptance* will determine the trajectory your life takes—that of unfulfilled or that of joy-filled.

Acceptance is the acknowledgement that right now, in this minute, things may not be what you want them to be. Daring 2B more is acknowledging your current reality, including your accountability for how it came to be, then invoking your superpower of intentional choice to do something to change the things within your control.

Acceptance is knowing, not thinking or wondering or contemplating, but knowing the only person, place, or thing you truly have any control over is you, your perspective of your reality, and the choices you make to affect it.

Consider your current situation for just a moment. What are the people, places, and things that are stealing your joy? Which of your behaviors, beliefs, fears, or tolerances are inhibiting your ability to grow or to manufacture and distribute a product of joy for God, others, and yourself? What are the roadblocks between where you are and where you want to be?

What is your accountability in the creation of your ecosystem? Is the business of your life, InJOYou, Inc., manufacturing and distributing a product of joy in every division that makes you, you? If not yes, then why not?

Your answers will reveal the opportunities for you to dare 2b more—dare to pivot, change, grow, and overcome the barriers between you and the joy-filled life you most want. Perhaps you need to dump the toxic boyfriend, go back to school, get into the gym, end a friendship that is stealing your positive energy and joy, spend more time with your spouse or your children, or take time for self-care, learn a new skill, pursue a passion, travel, clean up your money situation, or move. All it takes to change the trajectory of your life is the faith of a mustard seed, twenty seconds of courage, and one, small, pivot!

Your interpretation of the word "acceptance" is what will determine if you see a light at the end of the tunnel or merely an abyss of darkness. Will you choose the path of Bobby or Sue?

How you choose to accept the storms in life, like the people that hurt you, the unforeseen tragedies, the jobs lost, the empty bank account, or a seemingly endless series of roadblocks, will ultimately determine your ability to overcome them. How you see the world affects how you show up in it! When the storms come, as they always will, people naturally become vulnerable to negativity and all that comes with it, such as despair, anger, hurt, animosity, and disappointment. Your perception of those storms—Is this happening for me or to me—will determine where, to whom, and how you focus your energy. Your energy will determine if InJOYou, Inc., rides out the storm unscathed or crumbles in the face of the whipping winds and pounding rains.

DARE 2B MORE… BE ACCEPTING.

SDARE 2B MORE… InJOYou.com

Chapter 13

Footer 7—Mentors

Plans fail for lack of counsel, but with many advisers they succeed.
—Proverbs 15:22 (NIV)

One of the greatest values of mentors, is the ability to see ahead, what others cannot see and to help them navigate a course to their destination.
—John C. Maxwell

I met a young girl named Nadia. When she was around eleven, her parents introduced her to the sport of basketball. She loved it and was good at it, so good, in fact, that when she tried out for her first club team, she was invited to play with girls two years older than she was.

Nadia was a bit shorter than some of her other teammates. Still, because she played with more conviction and heart than almost any other player, her coaches consistently placed her in a starting position. Her most notable strengths included commitment, being a team player, a positive attitude, and coachability. Nadia practiced diligently and vigorously to become equal in skill to those with a bit more natural, God-given talent.

The first few years of her career were awesome; she learned a great deal and exponentially improved her skills.

Despite the coaches being uber-experienced in all thing's basketball, her club was still young; the teams struggled to win games consistently. As the club grew, so did the leadership's hunger to win. Winning became so important that the coaching staff dedicated the vast majority of their attention to a few select players deemed the club's top athletes. The light once cast upon Nadia began to dim, and with it, her self-confidence.

In her freshman year, Nadia's talent and drive secured her a spot on her high school's varsity team. Something about being on that particular court awoke the superstar from deep within her soul. Every time she stepped onto the court, she leveled up and found another gear, but more than that, she found her voice. Her coaches and teammates came to depend on her strength, encouragement, and leadership to win games.

After her first high school season ended, Nadia felt empowered and confident moving into the next club season, but something happened that changed her as a player and as a person; she got a new set of club coaches.

They, too, were uber-experienced, but they were also uber-competitive and, historically, poor losers. The more games they lost, the more the coaches focused their attention on their perceived "superstar players."

Despite being a starter for several years, this particular set of coaches did not view Nadia's talent with the same regard as the previous. The players who did not fit the mold of what a "superstar" looked like—tall—were frequently subjected to overtly negative and demeaning comments, inattention, and minimal gameplay.

Nadia valued her coaches' opinions and trusted their assessment of her abilities. The more they tore her down, the more she became afraid—almost paralyzed—to step onto the court. She feared making even a single mistake because, each time she had, the coaches approached her in anger and belittlement, including those times when the mistake was not hers to own. She couldn't bear the thought of being a source of disappointment for them or her team.

Consequently, the beautiful voice and decisive leadership skills, the talent she brought, and skills she embraced during her high school seasons all but vanished during her ensuing club career, leaving in their place hesitation and doubt.

The remaining three years of her high school career, she was a starter and a captain for the team under the direction of a far less experienced coach but one who took full accountability and responsibility for developing each player individually.

Coach Anne had a style that reached the heart of each individual. She understood the importance of coaching the mental game as well as the physical. Because of Anne's coaching style, Nadia felt empowered to fully embrace her gifts and talents—gifts and talents that led her team to championship brackets never before achieved in her high school's history.

Throughout her club basketball career, Nadia was subjected to coaches who did not value the importance of coaching the mental game. They placed more value on the win and the players they perceived were "superstars" than on developing and unifying the entire team. They failed to teach the players that individually, they were part of a whole, not the sum of the whole—none more valuable than another. The shorter girls who had to work harder took a backseat and, eventually, a bench seat!

Under the direction of her club's coaches, Nadia became a player consumed by fear rather than a player empowered to perform at her best. In high school, she took chances and left her heart and soul on the court no matter what. Coach Anne focused on Nadia's strengths rather than on her weaknesses. She created the space for her to become the "superstar" player she was always meant to be! At the other end of the spectrum, that same superstar player spent the better part of her last two club seasons on the sidelines.

What was different? Was she a bipolar player? Did her talent change between high school and club? No! Of course not! What changed was the style of coaching Nadia experienced.

Looking back, Nadia's parents recognized her club coaches had quite literally coached her love for the game right out of her heart. They did it by failing to recognize that the mental game was far more critical for Nadia than the physical one. In the last year of her basketball career, she no longer had a hunger for playtime; instead, she dreaded it. She felt emotional safety in supporting her team from the bench! When she got the opportunity to step on the court, she was so terrified of making a mistake that she didn't trust her ability or skills—those proven time and time again would help her team win games. She no longer found joy in playing the game she once loved so much; instead, it was a source of pain.

In her final club season, her team earned a spot in the club's first national championship. That victory validated that Nadia's club coaches' style was, in fact, motivational and effective for some. But for Nadia, that same style destroyed her ability to see herself as a competent and valuable player, not only on the court but off. She became an intimated and insecure player before she became a woman, very much the same.

The wrong coaches stripped her of something that had once brought her so much joy, but far worse was the impact their coaching style had on how she viewed her self-worth and value off the court! Their style changed how she showed up in every other area of her life!

We all need a mentor or a coach, but not all who can coach are equipped to coach everyone! The people you choose to surround yourself with matters; they are your teachers, tour guides, cheerleaders, reality checks, partners and investors, and keeper of the keys that can unlock the doors you dare to dream of opening.

Mentors are people who inspire, teach, and lead. You need a mentor/coach who can support you in bringing your dreams and goals to fruition by sharpening your God-given talents and strengths while honoring the values of respect, dignity, kindness, compassion, and humility.

Growing personally or professionally is incredibly difficult and exhausting to do alone. God did not create people to walk this life alone, nor should anyone want to! The fact of the matter is that life is just easier to navigate when you have a map! Mentors and coaches are your maps! But…and this is a huge but…not every person who has achieved success will, or should, qualify as the right mentor for you! The wrong mentor can lead you astray, destroy your confidence, and devastate your dreams just as quickly as the right one can empower you to climb mountains you have not even considered yet. A mentor may have the right experience, but the wrong style or values needed to lead and motivate you.

The right mentor is a person who not only has gone where you want to go but also can inspire the best in you to rise to the top. The right mentor will empower you to lean into your gifts and talents and challenge you to strengthen your weaknesses. They know how to fuel that burning desire within you—challenging you to dig deeper and find that next gear when all you want to do is quit.

Choose mentors who encourage your strengths, recognize your weaknesses, and support you in overcoming them without damaging your self-worth or inhibiting your competencies. A great mentor is a voice that makes you believe in yourself and the possibility and promise of your dreams. The right mentor will take you beyond the dreams you imagine today and open you up to a world greater than you can imagine on your own!

When you think mentor, do you automatically think in terms of your career, professionally or athletically? Most do, but you should not…at least not exclusively.

Allow me to pause and rewind a bit.

Recall that throughout this entire book, I have encouraged you to change your perspective—to view your life as a business purposed to manufacture and distribute a product of joy. I also mentioned that your business is comprised of multiple divisions, eight to be precise. The divisions of faith, relationships, careers, passions, creativity, curiosity, health, and finances combine to make you the person you are. Each division has the same purpose, to manufacture and distribute a product of joy. However, each division has different needs, requires different tools, and will also have a unique mission and vision.

Neglecting or denying resources to any of your divisions will inhibit the others' ability to manufacture and distribute a product of joy. Every division needs your attention on a regular and consistent basis. If you fail to care for any individual division, it will begin to produce weeds instead of joy.

Weeds have one job, to take over and choke out the life and health of everything that is not a weed. In other words, weeds are the people, places, and things that steal your joy! It is your job as the COO to define the people, places, and things that are like weeds that intend to harm the balance and harmony of InJOYou Inc. and to stop them from taking root in your ecosystem. If there are toxic people, beliefs and behaviors, activities or habits, jobs, or situations stealing your joy, then it is up to you to deny them the ability to continue to do so.

What does this have to do with mentors? Everything!

Generally speaking, most people are relatively "happy" in one or two divisions of their lives, but not in all eight. There are four primary reasons for this:

- Not having the know-how or resources to overcome joy-stealing obstacles.
- Denying that a problem or obstacle exists.
- Completely ignoring a division altogether.
- Placing little or no importance on building an authentically joy-filled life.

These are examples of self-created roadblocks and precisely why you need a mentor in each of the eight divisions of InJOYou Inc.

A mentor can be anyone who is three to five steps ahead of you, respects and honors the values you cherish and inspires your heart, soul, spirit, mind, and lastly, is willing to be your tour guide.

Let's say you have a fantastic marriage and do not feel you need a mentor in that area. First, congrats on having a fantastic marriage! Second, does fantastic have a ceiling or a cap? Is fantastic sustainable? Is your marriage *always* sheltered from the storms? Are you at risk of becoming complacent within "fantastic" and therefore missing the signs of stress? Is your marriage the only relationship that exists in your relationship division? Do you have children, friends, family members? What is the quality of each of those relationships? Is your entire relationship division, manufacturing, and distributing a product of joy? If your answer is yes, then you are right, you do not need a mentor, but you might want to consider being one for someone else! That is a great way to learn what you didn't know you still needed to learn. If your answer is no, then you need a mentor or coach who can support and guide your efforts to increase the production of joy in your relationship division! Remember, mentors, help you grow into the best version of yourself. None of us should ever stop wanting to be better for ourselves, the people we love, or God.

The proverbial yellow brick road was laid, brick by brick, by others who have already encountered and overcome the barriers that you may not have yet come up against. Mentors are the people who have acquired the wisdom and perseverance needed to avoid many of the pitfalls you are, or might, in your future endeavors experience! This is precisely why seeking out the right mentor(s) is a foundational footer needed to support a dare 2b more…life!

The bottom line is, none of us should ever feel that we are finished learning—that we have fully arrived! You will never get a credible plaque that says, "Congratulations! You have arrived at the end of knowledge!" Someone will always be a few steps ahead of you. That is a beautiful thing because, it means InJOYou Inc. has no ceiling and joy is never capped!

DARE 2B MORE… BE COACHABLE.

DARE 2B MORE… InJOYou.com

Chapter 14

Summary—ROI

I love historical buildings. When I consider what it took for our early ancestors to construct massive buildings and temples—that to this day marvel the minds of modern architects—I am in sheer awe! When I consider the limitations and barriers that the people who built structures like the Sistine Chapel, the Great Wall of China, the Leaning Tower of Pisa, or the Cliff Dwellings in Mesa Verde had to overcome, equipped only with the archaic tools of their time, it literally baffles my mind. How truly empowering is it, or should it be, to know that ordinary people used ordinary tools to build extraordinary things. If they were able to erect marvels such as these, despite seemingly insurmountable limits, just imagine what you can build with the plethora of resources available to you today!

Imagine when Giovanni dei Dolci was tasked with erecting the Sistine Chapel in 1473. I can envision him standing at the jobsite, contemplating how in the world he was going to pull off such a feat. He must have scratched and shook his head a thousand times as he gazed at the tools laid out before him. Perhaps more impressive than the actual construction of these marvels is that so many of them remain viable today. Perhaps the sustainability of these structures was a result of the builders' intentionality, fueled by a shared desire to erect a legacy, rather, than merely to build a structure! Perhaps the structural longevity was the consequence of their deep sense of personal accountability to honor those whom they served!

One of my absolute most favorite buildings is the Parthenon, which began construction around 447 BC. The temple's roof was supported by forty-six outer pillars and twenty-three inners, each 34.1 feet high. The pillars were the foundation for what was yet to be built! Today, many of those pillars remain standing.

What makes me love this incredible structure is that for the roof to be supported; every pillar beneath had to be intentionally built with unparalleled precision. If even one pillar was not up to spec, most likely, the other pillars could bear the weight of the roof. But over time, the added weight and pressure would result in stress cracks. Those stress cracks would continue to lengthen causing an inevitable collapse of the entire structure. Each pillar had to be built with an equal and intentional measure of care to ensure sustainability and longevity.

The dare 2b more…foundational footers are to InJOYou, Inc., what the pillars were to the Parthenon—the entire support system. They can stand alone, but together, they form an unshakeable foundation that can bear the weight of whatever is built on top of them. If one crumbles, then the others are weakened! If several crumble, then those that remain will not be able to withstand the weight atop them for long; eventually, they too, will fall! It is not a question of if, but when!

My ultimate goal in writing this book was to equip you with the tools to change your trajectory from unfulfilled to joy-filled. These seven foundational footers comprise the first step in building a life sustained by joy. The storms are certain to come as you dare 2b more…joy-filled. Still, when they do, don't be afraid! Dare 2b more… courageous—you are armed with faith, forgiveness, accountability, dreams, the superpower of intentional choice, acceptance, and mentors to help you rise, stand, and overcome anything that tries to steal your joy! Never forget that you were not created to be an employee in your own story!

I know what it is to live in pain, regret, shame, and hopelessness. There is truly little that is worse! I deserved better! You deserve better!

I have survived seas of agony, cried oceans of tears, and overcome seemingly insurmountable devastations time and time again in pursuit of realizing a life that was sustained by joy. Along the way, I collected a vast supply of priceless and irreplaceable tools—tools I used to build both stepping stools and, regrettably, stumbling blocks. My mission is to share my most valuable tools with you, in the hopes that you will use them to build stepping stools in your own life to minimize pain, anxiety, despair, and regrets. I deeply and genuinely want you to believe that joy is obtainable, *you* are meant to obtain it, and *you* are more than enough despite any circumstance, prior defeats, limitations, or the voices of others who steal your joy and inhibit your light from shining bright! It does not matter where you come from, what you have seen or done, whether your journey is just beginning, or you are starting all over.

There is just not a good reason to live a life of settling. There is not a good reason to spend your precious days chasing the *happiness drug*. There is not a good reason for you to not live sustained by joy! You can have the life you want but not without putting in the work to design, build, and maintain it! Regrets suck! That is the nicest way I can say it. You can build a life that will maximize joy and minimize regret if you choose too. You have that power. Own your superpower! Chase your dreams! Live on purpose, with purpose! Now that you know there is a better way; there is no excuse that remains for choosing to be an employee in the creation of your story!

You may not know this, nor believe me when I say it, but God *is* real. He is waiting for you and has never left nor abandoned you even it if feels as if he has. God loves you without limit or end! It is *his* greatest desire for you to know him and for you to experience the joy he always intended for you to know.

We are meant to live with a spirit of joy and peace. We are meant to use our gifts and talents to light not just our candle but the candles of those we invite to walk alongside of us, be they family, friends, coworkers, or strangers. Never let your light dim! The people you touch need to receive the gifts you have to offer. We are meant to live a life that honors Jesus.

It is my intention, desire, and greatest hope for you to realize and fully live your best possible life. As my kids would say, "You *do* you!" I want you to be non-negotiably, you! My hope is for you to step into your own best light and dare 2b more… freed from regret! I want to inspire you to dare 2b more…because a life of joy is worth it! I believe in you! Now all you must do is believe in yourself, make a choice—dare 2b more… Be faithful, forgiving, dreamful, accountable, intentional, accepting, and coachable!

I have gifted you with a set of tools crafted from my pain, struggle, success, and joy. The things I have laid out before you are not merely *my* ideas or theories. I was first invested in becoming the best version of myself before I challenged you to do the same. Just as I shared with you that as a photographer, I went before my clients to test the viability of the structure—to make sure it was safe for them—I have gone before you! I have done the work, and I continue to do the work, each and every single day God gifts to me!

I am living proof you can overcome adversities, both great and small, and that you too, can build a life of sustainable joy. I once heard it said, *if even one other person in my community has done something, then so can I.*

If I can rise up out of the ashes and build a joy-filled life of less pain and regret, then so can you! But I cannot do the work for you. I cannot motivate you to motivate yourself. I cannot create your ecosystem for you, nor can I tell you specifically what *you* need to dare 2b more…of. If you get really honest with yourself, you already know!

My mission was to give you another way, a better and more simple way to custom design the business of your life to maximize joy and minimize pain and regret. I taught you how to reframe your perspective from that of an employee to that of a powerful chief operating officer. I have hopefully empowered you to step into your best light and claim joy for yourself! Life is short! Do not waste yours knocking down the barriers that others who have gone before you have already knocked down!

In the corporate world, every member of the C-suite (CEO, COO, CFO, CIO, etc.) is charged with a level of accountability for the company's profit. The COO is accountable for honoring the CEO's purpose. Additionally, his responsibility is to custom design a corporate culture that can sustain the health and growth of the overall organization.

The COO must make intentional choices that will attract the right partners, who share a common goal and understanding that for all to profit, all must be united by the same purpose, vision, and mission. Understanding this, the COO will develop a road map that all who partner with the business must adhere to. The overall success of the organization is dependent on the design and maintenance of the corporation's ecosystem. The health and well-being of each and every member of the team must be taken into consideration. A healthy ecosystem will breed a healthy corporate culture, resulting in dividends of joy for all.

What is the purpose of a business—the real and raw purpose? The real and raw purpose of the business itself is to make money that will fund the lifestyle the founder desires! The business exists to make money!

Let us assume this is true; then it stands to reason that your life's business, InJOYou, Inc., also has one purpose, to generate a profit, so that you can have the lifestyle you want. What is different about your life's business and the business of your career or *job* is the compensation plan! Your *job* pays you money! That money then funds your happiness! InJOYou Inc., pays dividends of *joy*! That *joy* funds not only your emotional bank account but those of the people you love and care for, spend time with, work with, and generally come in contact with throughout your day to day living.

So, who writes your paychecks at InJOYou, Inc.? God will write your final paycheck, but until then, the people, places, and things you invite to partner with you at InJOYou, Inc., are the ones who will pay you in dividends of pain or joy. Which you receive will depend on the values and choices you make. You are accountable for both your pain and your joy; both are a choice.

If you are careless or reckless, or if you lack intention when choosing your partners, the people, places, and things that you invite into InJOYou, Inc., don't be shocked when they pay you in dividends of pain, anxiety, stress, depressions, or regrets.

The investment of your time, treasure, and talent should yield a return on your investment (ROI). You have invested your time and treasure into me by reading this book and trusting me to be your *joy tour guide*. In closing it is my plan to quickly bullet point your ROI for having invested in me!

- o You were gifted the secret scrolls to a joy-filled life I learned while traveling.
- o You learned about my journey to change the trajectory of my own life from unfulfilled to joy-filled.
- o You learned you are worthy of joy, regardless who makes you think or feel that you are not. You are a child of the most awesome God, and *he* says *you are worthy*!
- o You learned happiness is a drug that you need to stop chasing so that you can experience joy instead!
- o You learned what a dare 2b more…life is! In case you forgot…A dare 2b more…life means making choices that are so intentional your dreams have no other choice than to come to fruition.
- o You learned your life is a business, that of InJOYou, Inc., purposed to manufacture and distribute a product of joy so that ultimately you will leave behind a legacy of joy.
- o You learned you have a choice in being responsive or reactive. You can either live like a firefighter—always on the lookout for falling debris—or you can stop giving people, places, and things the power to spark the flame!
- o You learned the corporate culture of InJOYou, Inc., is affected by the ecosystem where your business is built. Are you wilting in the wrong ecosystem instead of thriving in one that was meant to support, grow, and sustain your joy?
- o You were challenged to consider the moments of impact that caused a pivot or change in your trajectory—from being the person you intrinsically want to be and were ultimately created to be.
- o I have shown you, through my eyes, the immense value of faith and the reasons for why faith is the lighthouse in your

storms—a light that can guide your every step, afford you boundless hope, and offer you comfort in the storms.
- You learned forgiveness is like CPR in your brokenness. I hope you have begun to take steps to make peace with all that needs to be forgiven, so you can set your gifts, talents, and joy free.
- You learned the difference between accountability of choice and accountability of consequence, confirming that consequences are far more palatable when you take ownership of the choice, before you take action. Are you demanding your choices honor your CEO, vision, mission, and values?
- You learned the value of dreaming and how hope and faith are the vehicle that will drive your dreams from idea to conception.
- You learned that your single greatest superpower is intentional choice. Intentional choices consider the impact they will have on the health of your ecosystem and that of others. Make your choices intentional and always in the light of honoring your CEO, values, purpose, vision, and mission.
- You learned acceptance does not mean giving up or resigning yourself to defeat or failure but rather acknowledging the truth of what is and then seeking opportunities to course correct.
- You learned the value and importance of having mentors in every division of InJOYou, Inc., but not just any mentor, only those mentors who empower your strengths and spirit, hold the space for you to be accountable to your goals, and honor your values.

So, now what? Well, what do you want? Who do you want to be? What legacy do you want to leave? Only you can answer the question "Now what?" You can either continue to be an employee in your story, continue moving in the direction of unfulfilled, or you can dare 2b more…and change your trajectory! You have the choice right now to continue living like an employee, waiting for happiness to pay you with stuff, or you can take a seat at the executive table! So, let me ask you... *What now?*

What if you choose to...

- ☦ Give God a chance to reveal how faith in him will transform every corner of your ecosystem! Truly, there is no reason not to know God exists. Look around you; there is nothing that exists in nature, including you, that was spoken into existence by any man. No person has ever created anything living from absolutely nothing at all. Allow space for both science and faith; after all, given God is the master craftsman of our universe, then it only stands to reason he anticipated, and intended for people to discover all that science has revealed! There is no greater hope than the promise God has given each of us in Jesus Christ. Besides, what will you really lose by trusting Jesus for your hope anyway? What will you lose if you try it Jesus's way? What will you lose if you are wrong in thinking Jesus is not real? (you know...other than your earthly and eternal peace and joy)

What if you chose to...

- ☦ Get wildly uncomfortable and forgive anyone whom you may begrudge, including yourself? What if you asked God to forgive you and others?

What if you chose to...

- ☦ Commit to being a person who is accountable for the choices you make, the ones you don't, and the consequences of both.

What if you chose to…

✟ Grant yourself full permission to dream wildly bold and fierce dreams and then set goals to bring them to fruition? What if you chose to be excuseless?

What if you chose to…

✟ Not make choices reactively but instead started to respond—to make intentional choices that moved you closer to the best and most joy-filled version of yourself? What if you were clear of what your values were? How might that one action change everything?

   If you do not declare and proclaim your values, others will force you to adapt to or adopt theirs.

What if you chose to…

✟ Accept that not everything will go just as you want it to go but that in every defeat lies an opportunity to try again? Sometimes the greatest blessings can only happen because things did not turn out as you expected. Remember acceptance is not giving in or giving up. It is acknowledging what is and then looking for the opportunities to change it. When you decide to take a trip, you must accept your airport may not offer flights to where you want to go. Does that mean you do not take the trip? *No!* It means you course correct and find a different airport!

What if you chose to…

✟ Stop thinking courage and strength and independence were swords of nobility, meant to be carried alone? We are not meant to do life alone nor can we or should we. What if you tapped into the resources around you? How could that change your life?

What if you chose to…

- Become an excuseless person who DARED 2B MORE… FAITHFUL, FORGIVING, ACCOUNTABLE, DREAMFUL, INTENTIONAL, ACCEPTING, and COACHABLE?

What if you DARED 2B…non-negotiably and authentically *you*? What if you dared to custom design the business of your life, InJOYou, Inc.? How do imagine it would feel and look to live a joy-filled life?

I have given you the tools to take the first step! Now I want to give you a resource—access to me! I am the instructor that can help you navigate the "What now?"

I have created a road map because when I took this road before you, I arrived at that very same question, *"Now what?"* What I did not have—what the experts had not told me—was *how*! I was desperate for someone to say, "Do this first, then this, then that…"

I did not want lofty ideas; I wanted applications. I wanted and needed a process! When I could not find one, I did what any entrepreneur does: I created what did not already exist. I created the Eco-Plan and the Eco-Print!

The Eco-Plan is like a blueprint. It tells the builder (you) *how* to build what the architect (*God*) designed! I created an intensive masterclass, intended to guide you through your moments of impact, help you construct the seven foundational footers, and create an Eco-Print. The Eco-Print is like an architectural rendering of a custom-designed ecosystem that can most optimally support you in manufacturing and distributing a product of joy in all eight divisions that make up your own unique business of InJOYou, Inc.

Once you see your Eco-Print on paper, you will not be able to unsee it! You also will not want to chase anything except your best and most *joy*-filled life! After I created my own Eco-Print, it took only eight months to erect! Unfortunately, I did not have a coach who had gone before me and could guide or support my journey, but you can! It would be my greatest pleasure and honor to be your *joy* tour guide!

I am not going to abandon you once your Eco-Print is complete; that would not serve you nor would it honor my personal life mission—to help you change the trajectory of your life from unfulfilled to *joy*-filled. After you complete the coursework and finalize your Eco-Print, I will take off my instructor's hat. I will be there to support you as you transition from where you are to where you want to be. I believe we need lots of different mentors and coaches! That is why I have a network of other coaches whose gifts and talents are different than my own. No one person has all the answers! If a coach ever tells you they do, get a new coach!

My goal is to support you in the very best way I can in your journey to build your life's business—that of InJOYou, Inc.! (Even if that means referring you to someone else.)

In closing, I want to thank you for your time, trust, and investment! I'm praying for your joy and that when you close the cover of this book, it will be the beginning of a new more joy-filled chapter as you challenge yourself to dare 2b more…by pouring the foundational footers of InJOYou, Inc.

For more information about how you can access my courses, coaching, or mentoring or to request me to speak to your group, please visit my website at www.InJOYou.com.

From the bottom of my heart, I thank you for your trust, time, and investment in your joy!

DARE 2B MORE… FREED AND JOY-FILLED!

About the Author

Laura is a faith-filled survivor and overcomer. The lifelong victim of overwhelming abuse, Laura was raised to believe that dysfunction was completely normal. Fighting and surviving with an unwavering hope that tomorrow would be better defined most of her days.

Laura has overcome abandonment, rampant addictions, tremendous loss, and all forms of abuse. Living in both poverty and wealth, being a teen mom, and a wife betrayed are only a part of her story. The power in her story is not in what she endured but in how she rose from the ashes to design and build a joy-filled life.

Faith and perseverance combined with personal and professional real-world experience have equipped her with the tools to serve her clients as a motivational coach and inspirational voice of hope, faith, and courage. Today, Laura coaches, mentors, trains, and speaks to teens and young women about how to custom design the *Business of Their Lives* to sustain joy!

Laura has founded or co-founded five successful small businesses including two portrait studios, a management consulting company, an alternative private school, and a promotional modeling agency. She's amassed over one hundred thousand educational hours in the areas of self-development, coaching, business, and leadership. She holds four professional coaching certifications. Over the past ten years, Laura has taught, coached, and mentored countless teens and women in the ways of confidence, empowerment, and joy! Laura's missional work has taken her to Peru, serving children impacted by human and sex trafficking, as well as into homeless encampments throughout our land. Laura's mission is to change the trajectory of ten thousand women and teens from unfulfilled to joy-filled! She has developed a proven blueprint for how to custom design the business of your life to sustain joy! For more about Laura, visit www.InJOYou.com @InJOYou.